Catchall

Doug Rucker

Catchall

By Doug Rucker
Layout by Helane Freeman

Copyright © 2021 Doug Rucker
All rights reserved

Doug Rucker
Vilimapubco
Malibu, California
ruckerdoug@gmail.com

No part of this publication may be reproduced, distributed or transmitted in any form or by any means, including photocopying, recording, or other electronic or mechanical methods, without the prior written permission of the publisher, except in the case of brief quotations embodied in critical reviews and certain other noncommercial uses permitted by copyright law.

For permission requests, sales to U.S. bookstores and wholesalers, or to inquire about quantity discounts, please contact the publisher at the email address above.

Library of Congress Control Number: 2021915794
ISBN – 978-1-7354717-4-7

First Edition
10 9 8 7 6 5 4 3 2 1

Printed in the United States of America

Catchall

Contents

Introduction 1
Laundry and Philosophy............................... 3
Walking the City Streets 4
Brain as a Tool 6
The Artist's Point of View............................ 13
Death and Reality 15
Rindge/Rucker Relationship......................... 17
Automatic Thinking 20
Dream of Flying Over Desert........................ 22
Body Surfing 24
Yes & No Philosophy.................................. 27
A Frank Philosophy................................... 31
Bus Stop 33
The Cyclist 34
The Red Truck 35
Destiny of Souls 36
Dream 37
Exhibition of Nothing................................. 40
Is There Life After Death?............................ 44
Matusak 47
A Springboard Dive Dream 56
Girl Guide Dream...................................... 57
Soul - Gary Zukov 59
Fingertip Dream....................................... 61
I Sing My Own Song & Other Things 63
Consciousness 68
I Owe Life Nothing 71
I See the World This Way 72
How Did You Get Into Reflection Photography?..... 74
Art, I Think!... 78
Life and Death... 99

How You Know You're Here	100
Remembrances of My Father	103
Movement of Continents	104
The Director	105
So What!	110
In Between	111
Soul	114
Common Sense Religion	118
My Philosophy	133
Reality	135
About Death	137
Christ Poem	141
I Clobber	144
Rider and Elephant	145
Stan Raymond	147
Black Hole	151
Soccer and Lost Dream	153
To Amanda	155
Car Crash in Fog	156
Raindrops on My Face	159
Will the Sun Come Up?	163
Marbles	165
Another Recent Episode	170
The Spider in the Sink	171
Over and Under	174
Secular Viewpoint	176
What and Why Pictures	182
Birthday Thoughts	185
For What is Thanksgiving?	188

Introduction

Catchall is a **catch** of **all** the variety of my past thoughts and philosophies, but until now unorganized. During the last period of years, I've been writing myself letters and essays about what's gone on in my mind about what I think and believe, with a little humor and a few dreams. However, such a variety of thoughts and ideas did not make a simple topic that would shape a book with a single subject.

Since I'm now pressed with new ideas and am inclined to make a new more cohesive book, I thought my former ideas and essays were important enough to be saved. I couldn't see them dying on a computer chip or wasting in some inaccessible notebook. I wanted to give them a bona fide life and let them be *"free to the world!"* to garner whatever brilliance or aversion would be their due. In three articles, *Body Surfing*, *Matusak* and *Raindrops on My Face*, I've taken former prose and presented them in poetic form. I thought them well-written and pertinent to the rest of the articles shown.

So, I invite you to read this book, and I will hope you are intrigued with what's presented, and accept it as one person's point of view. I know if you think differently, you were born with that privilege, and I value different points of view.

Laundry and Philosophy

While Marge was taking wet laundry out of the washing machine and putting it into the dryer, I walked in with my book and told her I was reading about *time*. It discussed whether God was making decisions *inside* time like all of us, or *outside* time like from an imaginary place beyond all eternity.

If God were *inside* time, he'd be as surprised as we all are by what the future holds, but *not omnipotent.*

If God were *outside* time, he'd be able to see the past, present, and future of all things and life would be pre-determined and therefore he'd *be omnipotent!*

But, what about free will?

If God is *outside* time and everything is pre-determined, there is no free will and God is *omnipotent.*

If God is *inside* time then God doesn't know everything and is therefore, *not omnipotent.*

At this point Marge put a wet towel over my head.

True experience of Doug Rucker.

Walking the City Streets

Walking the New York City streets
with hoards of people scurrying here
and there, my eyes fell upon a
stunning beauty walking toward me.

> She had a marvelous figure and an
> attitude reflecting dignity and brains.
> I was so taken I walked into an
> iron lamp post that knocked me
> unconscious and I fell to the ground.

I dreamt I was sitting in a leather
chair being lifted high in the sky.

> Reaching the top, securely seated,
> I descended almost to the ground,
> while seeing many joyful people
> walking in crowds below before
> being lifted once again into the sky.

An aerial view of the city told me I
was on a Ferris Wheel skirting the rim
of a vast ocean. Deciding to fly, I
leapt from the top of the wheel, spread
my arms and headed for Greece.

> At 30,000 feet and still breathing
> I ran into Albert Einstein still
> working in heaven and sitting
> behind a desk doing papers.

I swam through the air toward
him and shook his hands saying,
"Good job on your scientific work!"
Continuing, I came to Greece
and slid belly first into a field
of bright yellow daisies.

    In the distance was a castle and
    I made my way there and met
    Dorothy, Toto and the Wizard of Oz.

We sang a few verses of Over the
Rainbow before I leapt from a balcony
protruding from an uppermost turret
and sailed back to New York.

    Opening my eyes at the bottom of
    the iron post, was the beautiful lady.
    She said they were so worried and
    were so happy I'd regained consciousness.
    I thanked the beautiful, brainy lady.
    You see, she was my wife.

The Brain is a Tool

To understand my personal **Common Sense Religion** it's important to know the viewpoint I take when I observe the world. A religion or my personal life philosophy, or my own way of seeing things must view the whole picture. Viewing only a part of the picture allows me to remain in doubt as to what I might have missed. Anyway, *the greatest adventures lie within the realm of my own ignorance.* One such viewpoint is the difference between the **Brain,** the **Self** and the **Other.** It turns out the brain is not the self. See the following:

The brain is a tool.
It's not where we live.
The eye is a tool.
The ear,
the nose,
the tongue are tools.
The body's a tool. It runs.
It works. It plays. It propagates.

Where is the seat of the **Self?**
The toe?
The navel?
The center of the brain?
The elbow?
The buttocks?

Choose a place and there it'll be!

The lines of communication are the
nerves that run through the body.
The brain is the clearinghouse for

messages. It's hooked up to the power
source, but it's not the power source.

The brain is the clearinghouse.
The brain is the tool to be used by the ***Self***
to get what it needs for fulfillment,
for enrichment, for enlightenment.

The brain is the manager of the company.
It decides how to get what the ***Self*** needs.
The messages received by the brain
    are not always clear and many
    times are difficult to decipher.

Frequently the brain is confused by two
or more conflicting messages.
    I want an ice cream, but I'll miss the bus.
    I love soup, but there's a fly in it.
    I want to ride the bike, but it's got a flat.

This can give me a headache or backache or eczema
or hives or an ulcer.

Conflicts can lead to destructive habits
    like drugs,
    alcohol,
    smoking,
    overeating,
    undereating, etc.

Due to improper or no solutions, sometimes,
the will to fulfillment is severely discouraged
and sends conflicting messages to
    the chief,

the captain,
the inner person,
the ***Self***.

And the messages get scrambled in the
mind or clearinghouse resulting in
malfunction of the organism.

Growth and fulfillment are severely hampered
and the organism wallows and breaches.

The spirit is short-circuited.
Loss of power occurs. Correct
answers stutter and stammer.

When the will to fulfillment is overwhelmingly discouraged, the ***Self*** sends messages throughout the organism to the eyes, ears, nose, mouth, skin, liver, kidneys, nerves, blood vessels, alimentary canal, spleen, heart, brain, etc.,
    because the ***Self*** is suffering.

Since the ***Self*** is not the brain or nose or
intestines or genitals, where is it? It's
within in my whole person.

Without tools: eyes, ears, nose, skin, taste and
brains, the ***Self*** cannot, see, smell, feel, or taste or think.

Without a body it cannot run, jump, or play as
children do, for it is the ***Self*** that inhabits the body.

My ***Self*** owns my body.
My ***Self*** owns no one else's body.
My body, is an extension of my ***Self***,

and feels infinite power of an incomprehensible force.

The ***Self*** is why a being moves.
Its job is to feel; to see that the organism in which
it lives comes to fruition; to be born, to procreate and die.

The ***Self*** is not me and yet it's not anyone else.

Without the tools of my organism, my ***Self*** does not exist.

But, with my organism, I occupy the most significant
place, though I defy my organism to point me out.

I cannot see, hear, smell, taste or feel,
but my whole organism can.

> My tools can,
> my clearinghouse can,
> and, therefore,
> receiving these messages,
> I can.

My ***Self*** can.

My tools send the messages back to me and I feel myself.

Feeling is my calling.
I feel everything.
I feel sad.
I feel angry.
I feel anxious.
I feel loving.
I feel joyous.

I can feel these things singly, or all at once.
With my tools I can have multiple feelings.

I can feel lonely and in love.
I can feel sad and yet grateful.
I can feel fearful, yet hopeful.
I like to feel good.
I don't like to feel bad.

My organism knows which is which,
    though I cannot speak to it,
    and when I tell it,
    it's not in words.

When I feel good, I instruct my organism to continue
to do something to make me feel good again.

I control my organism, but like anything
mechanical, things sometimes go wrong.

    Should I burn my hand,
    my organism hurts and tells me.

I can feel foolish,
    or stupid, or regretful,
    or angry,
    or a combination of all my feelings
    depending on my attitude.

Oh yes! I have an attitude!

An attitude is the average state of feelings
depending on a conglomeration of feelings and
processing of forgoing and incoming messages.

Self begs the questions
>how did life start,
>or when was the beginning
>of consciousness?

Without warning, ***Self's*** were born into
a world with freezing temperatures, blistering
heat, windstorms, rainstorms, hurricanes, deserts,
tsunamis, earthquakes, starvation, lack of water,
animals hunting them, pandemics and
unimaginable hazards of every variety.

And each individual ***Self*** was born with a
variety of assets to properly cope. Of ten puppies,
there is the best and the worst. Of ten children,
there is the best and the worst. Of every variety
of living species, there is the best and the worst.

Add to that the variety of things that can go wrong
and go right, luck and lack of luck, happenstance,
for and against, and you have the difficulties that
living creatures must surmount to maintain their lives.

What inspired the first living organism
>to move,
>to spawn,
>to replicate?

After all the reading I've done in religious
>and scientific literature and figuring it
>out with ingenuity and common sense,
>I haven't the faintest idea.

What came along with the creation of

the *Self* might be called *"Other."*

*The **Other** is that which yields not but*
*   presses its burning way.*

The big bang expanded 13.8 billion years ago.
    The resulting Universe was created with galaxies,
    solar systems, stars and the indescribable
    miracles we see looking at the Earth and night sky.

And though it seems impossible, the entire
Universe sprang from little more than nothing.
It also seems impossible humans are born
with a striving for fulfillment and completion,
a penchant for life and a will to persist.
They contain a spirit of life beyond all comprehension
that is also relevant to all living beings.

The **Other** is the part without which
we'd be but clay. Where it comes from,
like the creation of the Universe, is in the
same category of impossible to know.

The Artist's Point of View

Go to any art exhibit and watch the viewers. Some of them lean as close as the guard will allow, their eyes inches away from the artwork. Others stand at arm's length taking in the whole picture and perhaps feeling the thrill of standing where the artist once stood to create the artwork on display. Still others stand way back or sit on the bench in the middle of the gallery and far away from the pieces on exhibit.

All these viewers know they will get different information about the picture from different points of view. Artists know this as well. Up close we work on detail, focusing on the small features of the subject that define some of its originality. Sometimes we become so involved with detail we lose our sense of proportion. The parts of the picture no longer fit with each other. That's when the middle and distant points of view become so important. As we move to the mid-length we may pay special attention to pencil application, correction in the drawing, layering and blending of colors, etc.

As we see artists at work we often see them moving back and forth from close to mid to distant points of view. A continuous conversation is going on between artist and his picture as he or she responds to what is happening on the page. But a major key to everything is seeing it from a distance. That is where the overall design of the piece comes on most clearly. At this distance we can see the basic areas of color, the general direction forming and the movement of the piece *(horizontal, vertical, diagonal, circular)*. We get a feeling for the full sweep of the piece and how different parts relate to one another and to the whole composition.

A Lifetime Point of View
Points of view are an important factor in our lives as well.

Getting mired in detail may happen both in our art and in our lives. What begins as a part-time pastime becomes full-time to the exclusion of many other important aspects of our activities. As we become more and more involved in detail we can lose sight of our whole picture. If we step back to the mid-length point of view in our lives, we can see that if there is something wrong we can open out to the broader picture. As a result of our new awareness our families, friends and communities become bigger parts of our life activities and we may or may not feel good about this new direction.

Less time spent in pursuit of ever demanding details can be spent in strengthening relationships, taking time for shared interest and involving ourselves in the service of others and the community. At the same time we may begin to wonder where the life-details are that made us the *life-art* we are.

It is at this point where stepping back helps. It gives us the overall picture. We can see the parts and the whole and how they work together. With a new life insight we can make necessary changes to bring ourselves back to balance where the close-up, mid-length and more distant views are that created the present whole.

Death and Reality

Death is where they throw you in a hole in the ground when you're done!

But, seriously, folks, that's what it is! It would be tough to say, just before you lay down for the last time, *"Hey! I missed what I was supposed to do! I didn't do it!"* Then the Devil would say, *"You go back to sleep! You shot your wad! That's IT for you!"*

Then I'd say, *"Git away from me, Devil! I didn't get to do what I wanted!"*

The Devil says, *"Yeah! Now it's too late! Ha! Ha! Ha! Ha! Ha! Ho! Ho! Ho! Ho!"* (The Devil's laugh booms out loud and strong!) He says, *"Just what I had in mind! I have worked a complete success on you since the day you were born. I slipped in your room in the wee hours of the morning and I gave you a TRAUMA!"*

The Devil goes on and on. *"Remember when you looked at the light patterns on the wall and they made eyes that stared straight at you, then turned into a horrible face? HA! That was ME! I was working on you! I used my MAIN TRICK! I call it FEAR! I use it all the time. Sometimes I use just a little FEAR every day. Then, when you are about half your life old, you got lots of pent up FEAR in you. You got FEAR you ain't even used yet! FEAR! That's what I say! FEAR is my best weapon! Ha! Ha! Ha! Ha! Ho! Ho! Ho!"* (The Devil's voice booms out loud and strong and ends in and unearthly shrieeek!)

FEAR is his trump card, he says. Well! I reckon it's so! I'd say that's what kept me from being *ME* most of my life. FEAR of what Mother would say; FEAR of looking inside myself; FEAR of facing my inner demons, FEAR of always telling the truth, *FEAR of REALITY!*

I could say, *FEARING REALITY* I refused its acknowledgement and turned instead to that which was not real. I did this so often, I became good at it. Eventually I couldn't see or face *REALITY* when it was staring me square in the eye.

Suddenly, outa nowhere I got hit! "WHAMMO!" "Holy shit! What was that that hit me?"

The Angel says, *"That's REALITY, dummy!"*

Me: *"Well, man, that hurt! Why'd you hit me? It felt like a brick wall fell on me. That was not nice!"*

Angel: *"I gotta get your attention, don't I?"*

Me: *"Why so hard?"*

Angel: *"You're so lost, I think you never coming back. You're so far from REALITY, I think you're goin' over the edge! For years, now, you only had one oar in the water."*

Me: *"Who are you, anyway, and why are you wearing that that black mask over your eyes?"*

Angel: *"Some call me ANGEL. Some call me THE LONE STRANGER! You can call me LONE!*

Me: *"What did you hit me with?"*

Angel: *"I hit you with the BRICK WALL OF REALITY! You SEE it now?"*

Me: *"Yeah! But I'm achin'!"*

Angel: *"You'll thank me for it later!"*

Angel rides off into the sunset on his white horse leaving a *SILVER BULLET*. Then, a man in a feather headdress who looks like an Indian comes galloping up riding bareback on a wild, brown mustang, with a wild mane flowing in the wind that says his name is TONTO.

Tonto: *"Where white man go?"*

Me: *"He rode off yonder into the sunset! What's this SILVER BULLET?"*

Tonto: *"That's A SYMBOL OF THE COURAGE TO FACE REALITY."*

Then the Devil comes up and says, *"You've been hit purdy hard, fella. Best you get to the bar, soak up a few and make it with a few dames."*

Me: *"Git away from me, Devil. With this Silver Bullet I'm gonna live in REALITY."*

Rindge/Rucker Relationship

In Boston, Mass, Fred Rindge Sr. made a huge fortune while 12 of his 13 children died of various diseases. The remaining sickly child, Fred Rindge Jr., lived, but was ill on and off all his life. Nevertheless, as a youngster with money he was able to travel, among other places, to Europe and the American west coast. In the shadow of the western mountains on one of his visits he met a Mrs. Preston, not a Dr. but a middle-aged lady healer who had penetrating black eyes with powerful beliefs and determination. Among the treatment of many rich patients, she helped Fred cure many episodes of his chronic illness by wrapping him with foliage, letting the chronic illness continue to infect and when it healed naturally, both the chronic illness and the infection were gone. He respected and admired her, and when she recommended a niece, May Preston, for a wife, Fred met her and married her within 3 weeks.

Fred Jr. made a fortune in the Los Angeles area and built a 54-room mansion within 3 miles of the present City Hall. Fred and May also bought the 25 by 1-mile naturally beautiful property now part of Malibu and intended to live throughout their lifetime in its pristine state. They built another large mansion at the mouth of Malibu Creek to enjoy their property and raise 3 kids: Merritt, Frederick, and Rhoda.

One of the most belligerent and troublemaking homesteading neighbors that gave the Rindges trouble, was Marion Decker, the mother of Charlie Decker, since they customarily used the Rindge's Malibu property to cross over to get to their own *"staked-out"* property.

One year, a devastating brush fire burned their Malibu mansion to the ground. May was convinced the homesteading *"troublemakers"* started the fire and thereafter held a permanent grudge against them.

After aiding Los Angeles by creating more businesses and money for the city and himself, Fred's chronic illness finally got to him and he died deep in an abandoned gold mine on Mount Shasta. After a certain mourning time, May formed the Marblehead Land Company to handle the many businesses owned by Fred Jr. and began fighting attempts by the public to build a road along the 25 miles of shoreline, the success of which was believed to totally ruin Malibu's pristine condition.

Their three kids, now grown, got married and had children of their own. Rhoda, May's third child, married someone named Adamson and she and her husband formed a very successful dairy called Adohr Farms. Adohr is Rhoda spelled backwards.

Efforts went for and against May Rindge, but when things improved she built a building to house the famous Malibu Tile Company that shipped tons of beautiful tile to rich construction projects all over the world. She began to make money and started another two-story, 54-room mansion on a hill overlooking her former Malibu house in Malibu Creek's estuary.

When the 1929 crash devastated the finances of everyone in America, May Kay Rindge, with all her businesses, suddenly found herself not earning money, but owing money. The construction of the mansion, half-finished with simulated carpets made of wonderful Malibu Tile, came to a halt and was later sold to the Franciscan Monks, becoming what is today known as the Serra Retreat.

To make money, May leased a mile of beachfront property adjacent and north of what is now called Surfrider Beach for those rich enough to have it as a weekend getaway. Later, she was forced to sell some of that same property, and hired Louis T. Busch, Sr. as the sales agent. The Marblehead Land Company drew up rules for sale to expire in the beginning of the year 2000.

Where I Come In

I was the only architectural consultant working for the Adamson's three children, Merritt, Rhoda and Sylvia. The mother, Rhoda Adamson, was the daughter of Fred and May Kay Rindge. I spent 4 years as the Marblehead Land Company Consultant.

My client for remodeling the Louis Busch real estate office was Louis T. Busch, Jr. Later, I was a free tenant occupying part of the second floor over Louis' office, with Malibu Surveyor Mario Quiros renting half of our second floor. For a short time, Louis and I were surfing buddies. Louis and his wife, Doris, sent me Thanksgiving candles annually for many years until Louis T. Busch, Jr. died in 2015.

I was selected as the architect for the Point Dume Mobile Home Park owned by the Adamson's children, doing the recreation complex, the pool, a four-unit apartment building, the laundromat and the garage and parking area. Curiously, the grading contractor was the late Charlie Decker, the son of the Rindge's former homesteader, *"trouble-maker"* Marion Decker.

Automatic Thinking

When I was a boy it was raining
in the back of our house. Big
droplets splashed on my forehead

> and hair and covered my face
> with smaller droplets, the ones I
> could lick off and still be smiling.

I remember rain with joy, even though
now that I'm old, I was happy with all
that existed; mainly my own existence
and the presence and wonder of rain.

> Sometimes I'd again like to be a
> child because rain brought peace,
> but that's impossible. So I sit
> here old and remembering days
> of the past wishing I were there.

Age has its bad moments, and
yet I'm glad to be alive while
also noticing the good and
respecting the circumstances.

> So what is an old person going
> to do while remembering his life of
> the past and thinking about the future?

I suppose it is to do what's in front,
because there's no alternative,
and so what is that, you might ask?

Writing and art are the only
things that come to mind,
plus devoting love to my dear
ones and others when I can,
be calm and carry on.

Dream of Flying Over the Desert

I find myself sitting several hundred feet in the air in what reminds me of a leather swing seat.
I suspect the ropes or cables on either side of me are connected to an overhead wing of some sort that holds me aloft.

There is an openly supported metal structure projecting in front of me holding a three-foot diameter, four-bladed propeller that spins and propels me forward.

I watch the scenery below, which is mostly unending sand that billows in some places and in others, rolls in undulations, like a washboard.

I travel like this for many minutes, or hours observing this interesting, but in the long run a boring scene.

Then I notice someone below driving a small, open-topped vehicle that's heading for a large trunked, baobob-like tree that stands alone in the vast, sandy desert.

Surprisingly, with his vehicle, he bumps straight into it and the tree topples over.

The *"someone"* gets out and tries to straighten the tree while its ridiculously wide trunk towers over him.

It then falls over the rest of the way and lies on its side, upended on the sand.

He goes to the other side and tries to *"right"* the tree, with success, and surprisingly the trunk plops easily into the watery hole from which it came.

The tree is standing upright again, but this time the trunk is even woodier and wider and the branches and foliage are thicker and accordingly adjusting to its new position.

I fly on.

There is more boring desert, but soon I see a green oasis in the distance.

It looks like a green island in wasted sand.

And as I approach, I sit in my sling-seat and lower myself to get a closer look.

Presently, I'm flying right next to the dark green foliage growing on 20-foot-high stone-like walls or fence-like structures visible through the side of the foliage. I fly right next to, in fact too close to the foliage and stone-like walls.

I'm now closer to the ground and precariously close to the stone-like walls when I awake.

What is the meaning of the dream?
Having looked at the National Geographic recently and seen the multitudinous configurations of sand, perhaps I had not internalized what I was really seeing.

Perhaps the dream helped me fly over this sand-covered land to internalize this experience.

What the tree and green *"oasis"* is, is still a mystery.

Body Surfing

Work was over and Tom and I were
body surfing the big ones on a short
beach in front of our business property.

> It was late fall when the ocean is
> warmest and we were surfing in
> the long twilight-hour after sundown.

At high tide the surf was big,
smooth and steady, and the oncoming
mound of water would leap and dance
crazily in the air before tumbling
to the sand in a rush of white foam.

> The breakers would slide down
> their own face, slam into the
> steep beach with a shudder and
> a sound that speaks of eternity.

The collapsed ocean would then
rush back out to sea with equal
power, and in the wake the sand
crabs would surface in a multitude
of little bubbles, feed and retreat into
their holes before the next seawater wash.

> The quiet, white, bubbling after-mist
> would hiss along the smoothing surface
> and I would taste the mist in my mouth
> and smell the salty air until on the
> horizon could be seen another big one

leaping and mounding for a repetition.

Tom and I would float up the big face
and decide on the spot, whether to slide
down for a thrilling ride, or having made
the wrong decision, go over the falls and
be slammed on our backs into the sand.

> We were slammed every other time,
> but we learned how to handle it.
> Anticipating a fall, we'd somersault
> and lay out flat, belly up, and become
> a victim of destiny, giving ourselves
> up to fate and the crashing wave.

Caught in a big shore break, I am
the victim. The surf does with me
what it will. Willingly, I give up control.

> The ocean has me. I am the ocean.
> The ocean is me! It feels like what
> I would expect being tumbled about
> in a cold-water washing machine.

Our knowledge of how to swim in the
sea; control when you can, give up
control when you can't. This rule
enabled us to escape injury.

> The cold sea was invigorating; the heart
> beat with enough power to warm
> the skin and equalize the cold
> would make the experience divine.

The cold was there, but we could resist it.
After an hour or so, when it became too
dark to see the oncoming waves and
our hearts were no longer equal to
the cold and we'd had our fun anyway,
we followed our instincts.

> They told us it was time to go in.
> Were I to do it over again? I would!

Yes & No Philosophy

In a discussion with a very close friend about the nature of the Universe, and though I felt the two of us had strong agreements on most points, I found my brain in question on other points.

One portion of my personal life philosophy is that all humans are different, but even so I understand that additional discussions still lead to new learning.

As a rationalist, I believe there are things that are irrevocably known like, Yes, something exists, or No, something does not exist. That being said, if Yes and No are so definite and unarguable terms they have to include words like Probably or Doubtfully. Probably Yes – or Probably No, something between Yes and No. If an agreement is to be made between opposites, anything not all Yes and not all No contains percentage points between the two extremes.

What came before the Big Bang? How do you make something as big as the Universe from nothing? It doesn't stand to reason. The experts don't know. When I ask them the answer is they do not know. Then I ask what is the percentage of Yes or No? There isn't any, only a variety of speculations. Do any of the speculations make sense? No more than the human imagination. So the answer is still irrevocably, No!

When I ask about life after death, there is no evidence that anyone has died and then come back to tell us how it was. Nor are there any tales of past performance of life after death. There are stories of Jesus, hypnotism, and scientific happenings enough to be called common, but no death as irrevocable as the roadkill of a raccoon I saw the other day on the highway. If humans come back to life, why cannot chimpanzees?

Without some evidence of past performance, humanity is no closer to the truth than fantasy. Can someone make a wild guess and it turns out to be the truth? Yes! Hurrah! But wild guesses are not considered common.

My friend might not agree that what I term a rational mind includes Yes that has irrevocable boundaries, and No with boundaries equally irrevocable. He must see that anything in between is a percentage of Yes or No. Yes and No are also synonymous with *Is!* and *Is not!* Yes and No are also symbols for True or False, Right or Wrong, Go or Stop, Jump, or Don't Jump, Cut or Don't Cut, etc.

If my friend doesn't see the irrevocability, or conclusiveness, or finality of the words Yes or No, then I'd have to agree he considers his own speculations as a bridge to what he'd prefer to think? Without the compulsory definition of Yes, or No, great elaborations are released for further imaginations, fantasies and speculations. Any of his other explanations are no longer forced between the two immutable extremes. We need these unchangeable definitions to make our thinking clear.

When the electric cord is cut, the light goes out. It doesn't stay on.

When the handle is turned off, the water stops coming out. The water doesn't keep running.

When diving in the water you get wet, you don't stay dry.

When jumping off a cliff, you hit the Earth a hundred feet down and die. You don't fly like a bird and continue life.

If we find ourselves with these natural rules universally true and part of the planetary foundation of this miracle planet, wishing it were otherwise isn't living in the real world. These immovable facts, universally true, provide a dependable environment that makes it possible to eat, work, make love and continue the species. Without these permanently trustworthy rules, we'd be lost. These continuing facts, or conditions have produced and maintained every living being that exists. To have it otherwise is to abandon what the entire universe continually shows us.

Somebody could say, *"Well, Hell! I could have told you THAT!"* Then why did I bring it up?

Yes & No Philosophy

Because I observe throughout the world, many human beliefs are contrary to the Yes/No rules of the Universe. For many, the earth is a place where Yes and No truisms are ignored. The Universe's idea of Yes and No are often thought to be the opposite. Yes is No! No is Yes! And where there's disagreement with the language, disagreements between humans naturally and always occur.

There can no longer be a percentage between adamant, unchangeable fact and another adamant unchangeable fact because neither of the opponents agrees the adamant fact is unchangeable. If one classifies a Yes as a No, and No is a Yes, and another believes a Yes is a Yes and a No is a No, how can you have a percentage between the two adamant, unchangeable facts when it seems both are changeable.

This non-agreement leads to fantasies and speculations that are considered truths as if the theory of irrevocability of Yes and No never existed. Miracles, and portions of most religions set an example with Christ coming alive after dying on the cross in the light of literally billions of experiences opposing life after death. Christ rising after death in the midst of billions of lasting, non-returning deaths isn't reasonable in the 13.8 billion year experience of the Universe. Where is a corroborating past experience of anyone coming alive after death?

So-called miracles, conceived by recently existent humans, go directly against the Universal Laws of nature. That means the grand power of the entire Universe that developed over billions of years contain rules and regulations that are minimized and changed by recently materialized humans into something totally adverse to everything the ancient Universe taught. In the history of the world's religions the vast number of people believing a single person, like Jesus, can come back to life, or that Life and Death are interchangeable does not make sense.

Add this to the beliefs in historical myths and other so-called facts against the Universal Laws of Nature, and you have some idea of why huge sections of humans can't agree and must, among other things, hate each other and fight unending wars. This is why humans have no agreement as to what are the irreversible qualities of Yes and No, or Up or Down, or Jump or don't Jump.

Great sections of our human species don't agree on the basic lessons of the irrefutability of Yes and No taught by the Grand Universal Force! If they did, we'd have much more to agree upon.

A Frank Philosophy

Note: Under each circumstance my houses are the best I can do. I don't have to establish myself. I'm already established. I only take jobs that allow me to express what I believe, not only about construction, but life as a whole. I'm in love with my work. I do everything myself: program writing, design, working drawings, specifications, contractor selection and supervising work once a week. I make good houses and if you build one, I think you'll enjoy what we both have created.

I don't like the idea that a house has to be ostentatious or eye-catching or have some kind of curb appeal. I don't do that. I try to build a beautiful house fitting sensitively into its site; one the owners are proud to own because it conveniently accommodates their personal way of life; one they like to come home to because it's beautiful, convenient to live in and everything they love is there.

I don't believe *people are for houses,* but *houses are for people*. Many clients have to adapt themselves to the architect's intricacies. In our house you will not have to do that. Our house is an understated background for you, your children, guests, activities, books, music, artwork, furniture and anything else you'd like to bring into it. The new environment will not intrude upon the senses, but if it is chosen at all, it is quietly beautiful; an environment where a sudden delight of the senses awakens you to how lucky you are to be in the place you are.

Some houses look as if the architect was forced to establish himself in his own eyes and, therefore, in the eyes of others. They are usually showy and pretentious. *(One example would be a house near the ocean in the shape of a wave, or a house in the mountains that looks like a boulder.)* I'm tired of looking at them. I wish they'd go away. In fantasy if not in actuality, my houses love secret places; they're lost in the woods and covered with vines; gone from the world and the owners are snug and secure in love with their place and where they are. This is my idea of what my house will do for you.

Bus Stop

Have I died and gone to heaven?

Or perhaps I'm dreaming!

Has this angelic bus

taken me to my heart's desire,

or is this an arbitrary spot?

Nevertheless,

before I died, or fell asleep,

I wanted to shop.

And this angelic dream bus,

a method of movement

for sleeping or dead,

has taken me where I want to go.

If shopping it is?

So be it!

For in dreams or death,

I know in my soul

living or dead,

what I desire will happen.

Doug

The Cyclist

With a hulk of blue and a slash of red,

he has places to go and things to do,

but is trapped by art.

Carrying baggage

frozen in time,

he flees his rigid life.

After many years,

his struggles are personal

and he is guilty and anxious to return.

Either that,

or he is a figment of our imagination,

an hallucination

that feeds our mind,

a sort of vision

from which there is no escape

that follows us around,

interminably.

Doug

The Red Truck

After a hard day's work,

we see the **Red Truck** resting.

Has the owner stopped for a sandwich

or maybe a beer?

Or has he returned in the truck

from a trip through starry skies

and visiting our Galaxy

to Mars, Jupiter and Venus?

But it's good to be home

and park the **Red Truck**

and have a sandwich

and a bottle of beer

and relate his tales

to old friends

like you and me.

                                 Doug

Destiny of Souls

Prologue: This is a series of thoughts and perhaps a question or two about Dr. Newcom's book called *Destiny of Souls*.

Dr. Newcom is a certified hypnotherapist and has regressed people, not only back into their young lives including the womb, but further into a place before they were born called *"between lives."*

Patients under hypnosis tell him that they have been reincarnated thousands of times and have lived thousands of different lives; that their past lives were good or bad depending on their own *"in-between"* life choice they made having been influenced by their lives lived immediately before.

Though when their spirit after about three to four months after impregnation enters a new child to be born, they have amnesia and forget their former lives.

He reports that his clients say they are given a preview of the future of the newborn child they are to inhabit and they have the opportunity of choosing the next life according to what they have to learn or what they need to achieve in their following lifetimes.

After death, the spirit of the person goes to a place between incarnations, or between lives, to give comfort to grieving loved ones, or to complete unfinished spirit-business in their spiritual lives. He calls this an *"in-between lives"* existence. I'm left with questions.

Dream

I'm supervising a job in the north end of Malibu near Trancas. I pull up in my car. Mike Meru is handling the grading work, messing around with the dirt and making an entry with retaining walls. I have minimum work on this trip and have just come from supervision of a smaller Malibu job.

I look up from the private street between dirt and forms and see my client returning. She's healthy, thin and resembles a former client of mine, Bambi Young. Though I don't see them, I'm aware that one or two small children run past into the existing house. I suspect their ages are about eight and nine. My client's head is decorated in a strange way. It looks like it's been sprayed with white paint or dusted with talcum powder or white chalk. Her hair is frizzy and the makeup around her eyes makes her look like a clown. I assume she's just come from a costume party and I try in vain to recognize her.

Just before leaving, I notice my daughter, Viveka, standing above me on the graded path. She is wearing a printed dress, beautiful and in a deep blue. We acknowledge each other and I'm surprised she is helping Mike Meru on *"grading"* work in those clothes.

Then I leave to go back home or to the office. On foot, I enter a big, round concrete tunnel, perhaps 16 feet in diameter, and it descends at a steep incline, dropping perhaps 20 feet in 60 feet. I can see the dusty, descending, slightly curved walkway leading down to the bright, round shape of the tunnel's end. I suspect this will lead to my car, but when I reach the bottom I discover green weeds and trunks of small trees or brush as if along a deep barranca. There is water rising in the barranca, and coming up the narrow pathway leading down, is water bubbling up. This is not the way to going outside or the car. Rising quickly, the water enters the end of the tunnel and I immediately retreat up the tunnel keeping ahead of the growing water.

A local man appears alongside me. He seems to know about the big tunnel's round, circular end, the barranca and quickly mounting water. He seems pleased to lead me back out and I follow him back up the tunnel.

At the top of the tunnel he goes up into a confined, rising, cylindrical space, approximately five feet in diameter that rises, evidently, to the surface, the street and my car, etc. He has disappeared and I assume he has already made his way up the destroyed circular stairs. I am left to negotiate broken, rotten, metal circular stairway treads. With each step, I have to support myself by stepping on thin, and I assume, very rusty leftover portions of the treads until I get to the top. The treads are almost invisible in the dark light and I'm not clear they will hold me, which makes it ever more difficult. I have no knowledge of stepping into daylight of *"coming out of the hole",* but do have a flashing image of daylight and foliage indicating I got out.

End of Dream

I awake, still semi-dreaming, and have a head pop. *(A strange sound in my head created by blood vessels? I don't know.)* I've had many of those in the past, but have not had them for a long time. I do not want another stroke.

The morning is misty/foggy and there is water on the concrete outside. I was awakened previously with stopped up nostrils and had to get up, blow my nose, and poke Vick's VapoRub up each nostril.

What is the meaning of the dream? I'm 82 years of age. It is probably the quickening of old age. The older I get, things are harder to do. On Saturday, I had a long walk and talk with Viveka. Feeling her age with dizziness, Marge, when she stands, has diabetes, age tremors and a continual need for sleep.

In the future, Marge and I will take up whatever slack that's needed regarding our life and relationship. I worry if I'm incapacitated with a stroke or ill health, Marge, though intensely willing, won't have the energy to face whatever problems occur. *Allowing the scroll of life to unroll* means resolving problems to the best of our ability while enjoying our blessed free time.

Exhibition of Nothing

I was leafing through Kirk Varnadoe's book about new American abstract art of the 21st century called *Pictures of Nothing*. In it, there is a picture of an installation called *Iron Floor Box*. It's painted brown and is very big, about 4' high x 7' wide x 10' long. Even though it's in his book called *Pictures of Nothing*, I guess it's actually a picture of *something*. After all, it IS a box. Wow! A big iron box! There's no open able top, so it may not hold anything, and it's so large and heavy I could never put it in the car trunk. In fact, to move it, I'd need a forklift.

There is another installation called *Scatter Pieces*, where a great number of little white pieces of foam *(like packing corn)*, each about 1" long, 3/4" wide and 1/4" high, have been thrown by the thousands all over the floor. This is in an art museum! No walking in that room! Just looking and wondering why this should be there at all and asking myself, *"What kind of person would do this? Don't let the kids in that room! The cleanup guy quit. Am I missing a statement of some kind? Is the artist a genius and I'm too dense to understand the ultimate significance, the root symbolism, the underlying core of what he's saying – or not saying? Or is this a humorous prank?"*

But I love art and continue through the *Pictures* book, and come to a huge metal sculpture occupying the entire central atrium of the Corcoran Gallery of Art in Washington, D.C. It's called *"The X."* Looking down from the colonnaded balcony, the immense black, metal "X" must be 20' square, 10' deep and 2' thick. It had to be welded together in its present location because it would be impossible to bring it in through the front door. I came to the conclusion; *"Yep! It's an "X" all right. Painted black, too! There's no doubt about it, it's a positive statement of some kind or other! Surprising, too! To see a big "X" taking up the entire interior atrium with a surrounding balcony for observing the symbolism of whatever it symbolizes. "X" certainly marks the spot!*

That brought to mind an idea. *Exhibition of Nothing.* Though Varnadoe's book is called *Pictures of Nothing,* if I could rent a museum, I could put on an art show and call it, *Exhibition of Nothing,* wherein the title clearly expresses what's inside.

"What you see – or don't see – is what you get! Enter for an experience the likes of which you've never seen. In fact, in 'Exhibition of Nothing,' you may never see IT! Come inside with me as I open the high double doors and walk jaunty-jolly into the gallery to see – or not see - Exhibition of Nothing."

What greets me is a well-lighted, 15'-square blank canvas. It's pristine in its size, shape, and cleanliness. A side note on the wall invites me to see within its strong white boundaries anything I want to see. I'm encouraged to use my imagination and create my wildest hopes and dreams, or my greatest fears, or a vacation on a South Pacific island with a beautiful starlet, or aunt Mary on a skateboard, etc. I blank my mind and use the canvas for meditation. Then something drifts in. I immediately see clouds forming and rolling and forming. Eventually they evaporate, revealing nothing, and I'm ready for another art experience.

In another room, I see a big wooden box with a beautiful handle that's inviting me to open. Other curious art patrons gather around to see what wonderful things may be in the box. I lift the lid. It's empty. I see the top, sides and bottom. It's made of smooth, slim pieces of polished hardwood, but there's nothing inside. Then I notice, on a pedestal beside the box, a note that says I'm to *imagine* what's inside and that's my reward. I imagine it's filled to the brim with $100 bills and turn elsewhere for another divine art experience.

I notice an archway over the top of which is a sign, *Another Experience!* I walk into a room through the arch. There's nothing on the other side! The walls are bare. The hardwood floor is clean and polished, but with nothing on it. I look for paintings. There are none. I look for a mural on the ceiling, but see only white plaster and indirect lighting.

Naturally, I find a note that says, *"This room contains whatever you can imagine."* I'm sick of trying to bring whatever I can bring to it, so I imagine 100 beautiful dancing girls and move on.

I come to a miniature room with a single glass door. To the side it says *House of Fragrance.* "Experience bouquets, aromas, perfumes, and scents that will delight your nose." I open the glass door and inhale deeply. It smells like regular air. There's no wonderful whiff or engaging tang, but stale air. Then I notice a standard sign that says, *"Dream up your own scent and return to the gallery feeling good about yourself."* I call up the scent of hot coffee, toast, scrambled eggs and bacon and realize I didn't have breakfast. The thought of something to eat I have to admit is particularly engaging. So far, I've enjoyed the art show. Let us go on to the next *Exhibition of Nothing.*

The next room contains several colored lights focused on a pedestal that holds a hologram of a piano keyboard. It says, *"Play the piano."* I step into the hologram and strike my fingers on the keyboard, but they go right through. It's like playing on air. There's no sound! I try again. No music! No hum, no clatter, no bells, no noise. Nothing! Just frustration and thoughts; *I'm wasting my life.* I look for other instructions and obviously find them! *"Pretend you're playing the piano and you can hear anything you want. This is your reward."* Apparently, in this wonderful show, whatever I bring to the artwork is mine to keep. I imagined playing the song, *Darktown Strutter's Ball. (I'll be down to get ya' inna taxi honey. Ya better be ready 'bout ...)* I see! Whatever I bring to it is what I keep!

I'm bored! I decide to take Marge to the cafeteria and get coffee and donuts. We sit down and order. The waitress brings us a couple of empty plates and unfilled white cups and says,

"Enjoy." Of course, I realize we have to imagine the taste of the bacon and eggs and toast and jelly, and thrill to the imaginary steaming-hot coffee. When she brings the check for $12.57, I cross out the numbers, sign the check and throw down a couple of invisible dollars for a tip.

And so, our trip to the *Exhibition of Nothing* was a fine day. I look forward to the time when it returns. After all, I briefly got to imagine the unimaginable on a blank canvas, see a fake boxful of $100 bills, experience in my mind a room full of scantily-covered dancing girls, smelled a wonderful breakfast, and recalled one of my favorite songs. Afterward, we had a magnificent breakfast located only in our mind, and left a big imaginary tip for our waitress.

Our schedule did not allow us to visualize a brilliant story while trying to read a novel with blank pages, or imagine the brilliant work of sculptors in a room of empty pedestals, or be entertained by performance artists with no performers. Perhaps next time.

Is There Life After Death?

I've been reading Deepak Chopra's book, *Life After Death*. I'm well along in it, but haven't finished it yet. When Tom asked me about it, I could have said I agreed with Chopra and believed there was life after death, or I could have disagreed with Deepak, and said NO and thought his idea poo-poo, or I could have said my solution was in between and divided into likely or unlikely with required percentages.

I told Tom obviously, I couldn't answer until I'd finished the book. In an attempt to answer the question, is there life after death, at this point I'd agree. There IS life after death. Even after an extinction of most species on earth, there has always been a small percentage of life on the face of the earth. Therefore, YES, there is life after death, maybe not for people, or 135 million years of dinosaurs, but maybe in general for a haphazard number of a few earthworms, bacteria, or certain underwater fish, or lions, tigers and bears, but no return to the once-in-a-lifetime individual characteristics of each once-living individual creature.

The question really is after death, will our particular person, you or me or any living creature with their individual characteristics, remain alive, and does the species survive? Or will there be some kind of consciousness resembling and related to each living being exist after death.

(Yes! No! Maybe? What percentage do you think? How long would it last, 10 billion years, 8 billion years, 3 billion years? In that lost time before the big bang? After the universe has dissipated?)

A year ago I had a pacemaker replacement during which they gave me a drug to eliminate that brief portion of my memory that might have experienced pain. It worked perfectly. I can remember everything before and after, but have no recollection of pain or the operation.

Despite the possibility of our planet being hit by another comet destroying all life of any size whatever and by any stretch of the imagination, will we yet retain the experience of being alive after death, or will, like the miracle-medical drug above, take place and our memories are lost to the cosmos? After death, do we remember that period of our lives while under drugs or asleep? Do we remember pain? Do people instantly exploded into less than dust when hit by the Hiroshima atomic bomb continue to live after death?

I think the answer to the question, "*Is there life after death?*" is similar to the question, "*What's inside a box that can't be opened?*" Until we open the box, we don't know what's inside. I believe in Near Death Experiences. Too many people have reported them not to be a common truth, but, of course, the people reporting them weren't dead like the remains of a raccoon on the highway having been hit by a car. I don't know if chimpanzees, or gorillas, or dolphins, let alone squirrels, mice and earthworms, are somehow alive after death. Chimpanzees have 96 percent of the same DNA as humans. It seems if humans experience life after death, at least chimpanzees might have made the cut. Where is the cutoff point for life after death regarding feelings and practical events that have occurred in ants, bees, plants, fish, birds, bacteria, molecules, amoebas and viruses?

A side note: The above items are ignored in Chopra's book. Since homo sapiens, as we know them, hadn't arrived on earth until about 80,000 years ago, when there was no human history or language to exchange thoughts, where was life after death then? No humans, no life after death! Is life after death true only for sudden, born-in-the-wink-of-an-eye humans? If it isn't true for all living things, why is it true for just humans? Is life after death true for all living things, trees, plants and ocean algae, including frozen organisms when our earth was encased for 100 million years and known as the ice planet? Did human souls exist before there were humans? There seems little conversation or study on life after death for anything other than humans. Will they (we) be here after our sun blows up and our whole solar system is gone?

A method of decisions involves bins. The first is a Yes Bin containing every fact of which we are sure. The second is a Maybe Bin including a percentage of what we suspect might be so. The third bin is the No Bin or whatever is definitely not true.

In conclusion: There isn't any.

Matusak

There was a neighborhood girl my age,
who was quite attractive at 13,
who walked by our windows quite often.

She strode purposefully forward,
straight as a willow
carrying her books in front,
hair loose, responding to each stride.

She was well groomed
and had a special dignity
which I admired.

In fact, she was conspicuously
the only eligible neighborhood girl
and Mother couldn't understand
why I didn't get to know her.

*"Why don't you invite Antoinette
to the movies? She's attractive.
You'd probably like her. She
comes from a nice family."*

I'd refuse, but reluctantly,
or I'd put it off until later;
I wanted to know her,
but my fears were too great.

I wouldn't know what to do or say.
I thought I had no ideas.
Small talk didn't seem appropriate.

Why should she care what I thought?
What did I think, anyway?

I was mostly afraid of life.
I couldn't speak in class.
I was afraid of bullies across the park.
I was afraid of getting into a fight
with some tough gang kids.

And instead of being the victor,
I'd do it in my pants.
I was afraid of failure.
Did she want to hear this?

I was so self-centered,
self absorbed, being
in the agony of adolescence,
I couldn't act.

I was troubled because
others my age seemed
to have no trouble at all
with the opposite sex.

In fact, the opposite sex
actually seemed to enjoy
their transparent advances.
Some of my friends
didn't take girls seriously
and they had a line.
What was my line?
I didn't have a line!
I didn't like lines.

Some of my friends
who were negative people,
used girls for themselves
and the girls didn't seem to care.

Or were they just unconscious?
How could I use people,
especially attractive young girls
I respected?

There was much female thinking
in my head at thirteen
partially because my only verbal
communication was with Mother.

Dad was non-verbal,
apparently had no philosophic ideas,
didn't read books,
or like classical music,
or ballet
and had little time left
after his two jobs.

Dave was four years,
three months my junior
in the fourth grade!
I couldn't talk life with him!

I was too shy to bring up life
with my fellow students.
I didn't like some parts of life.
I was afraid of life.

Teachers frightened me too;
were swamped with kids anyway.
Families are a dynamic
I learned at 50,
from a book,
The Family Crucible,
by Napier and Whitaker.

Members play their parts
and have little control
over the dynamic.

My painfully shy Mother
might have married
someone who loved
more of the things she loved.

Someone who appreciated
classical music, journalism,
fine books, ballet,
and the intellectual life.

But for other reasons,
she picked Dad
who liked cowboy movies
and gangster shoot-'em-ups.

Being somewhat afraid
of the outside world,
constantly retreating into her books,
having only the non-intellectual
Ruckers for personal association,
to whom could she reveal her true self?

Me, of course!
I was the special one
who was the recipient
of no less than prenatal influence.

I was the one who received
her idealistic stories
about princes and princesses,
the value of honesty, diligence,
perseverance and the qualities
of the true conqueror.
I sought to live the American way,
as a Superman
brandishing the American flag.

Though I am lucky
to have learned about
these things and believe in them,
still I was a captured audience;
part of the unconscious family dynamic.

I received them solely
from her point of view.
I listened to her female dreams
and philosophies
and was the one involuntarily
available to incorporate
her personal preferences,
ideals, inadequacies, fears.
Part of me understood her
and the idealistic stories
and appreciated her for them.

Part of me loved her
and projected her imaginary
female so high on the pedestal
she was unattainable.

Women were perfect and ideal.
They were the ones
for whom to do manly things,
be dependable, bring
home money, take charge
of things, be responsible.

Women were the adored ones,
the ones, who if you were
to split the arrow, as
Robin Hood did,
could be won or achieved,
much like Dad had acquired Mother.
How could I split the arrow?
I had difficulty chewing gum
and walking at the same time.

I thought I understood
the female personage
from the female point of view –
Mother's.

I had no big brothers like
Sam Keen describes in
Fire in the Belly,
or Aaron Kipness
in *Knights Without Armor*
or Robert Bly in *Iron John,*

giving me some form
of the male ideal,
telling me the male facts of life.
My many uncles were
blue collar workers
who apparently did
without deciding what.

They were not into deciding
how to live or developing
the proper philosophy of life.
You went to school,
you got a job, got married,
raised some kids and retired.
They led the truly unconscious life.

Was it worth living?
It is true, Mothers can give much,
but they can't give the same
things a father can give to a boy.

I learned invaluable man things
from Dad, but they were not in
words or in the realm of the intellect.
They had no anxiety attached to them.

They were not challenging or urgent.
He had no ax to grind or point to make.
He had no desire to live through
his son the way an intelligent Mother,
as was typical in those days, had to do.

I learned to love by watching him love.

I learned to work hard because he did.
I learned it's OK to like what you do
and not like what you don't.

I learned good common sense.
I learned to be meticulous
and funny, because that's the way he was,
and I learned to value women
as precious people, every
bit an extension of God as
anything else, because Dad did.

However, this was beyond me then.
I was just caught in the family dynamic.
So, I didn't talk to Antoinette.
I didn't get to know her.

I didn't know her idiosyncrasies
that might have pissed me off.
I didn't know if she was an angel
capable of abiding love.
I didn't know if she was smart
or stupid or had any particular
ideas about life.

I don't know whom she married,
or whether she was a good Mother
or what her other specialties were,
or whether she aged fast or slowly.

I don't know whether she died
of an unusual disease
or yet lives and can tell me
some soulful stories.

I was too afraid to pick up the stick.
T. S. Eliot, in part of his poem,
The Love Song of J. Alfred Prufrock, says:
*"I have seen the moment of my greatness flicker,
and have seen the eternal Footman hold my coat,
and snicker, and, in short, I was afraid."*

A Springboard Dive Dream

At 3 or 4 AM while sleeping I dreamed an elderly woman was standing stiff and straight on the high board of a swimming pool in preparation for making a dive off a three-meter board into the swimming pool. She waited an interminable time, evidently consolidating every physical manifestation she'd need to make the perfect front dive.

Eventually, she did so. Note: All divers lift one of their knees high while approaching the end of the board so that when both feet are returning they can drop by gravity to exert the most force depressing the board down to its utmost to accentuate the board's lift that sends them high into the air. Then they will briefly pose for the essence of their dive before plunging forward to execute a perfect non-splash entry.

She didn't lift the knee or get the preliminary height before she fell flat off the end of the board, and landed full length, flat on her face and stomach on the surface of the water making a great splash. Surprising myself, I broke into a burst of applause, evidently in appreciation for the dive, then immediately asked myself why I was clapping for such an imperfect dive?

I answered myself; I gave her applause for a person of her age to have the courage to make a dive off the high board in the first place. There were a few more arguments here and there before I could let the curiosity go, but eventually I forgot what they were.

The reason I had the dream at all might be to reinforce at my own age of 93 to have the courage to continue writing and producing some kind of work.

Girl Guide Dream

(About a disconcerted man and a young girl with an indescribable mass between he and a single tear (from crying) on the other side.)

There was a young lady in her college years, let's call her Mary, who was attractive and employed to lead Mission visitors on Sunday tours. A student of Father Serra's life and early California history, she loved Missions and her new job as guide.

Her overseer, Father John, was worried that Sunday because Mary was not her usual self. It was not clear why. Perhaps she had a boyfriend disagreement, or an illness in the family, or a bad hair day.

An art-therapy sort of picture of the situation would be like this: on the left, hands on hips and looking concerned, is Father John. On the right, with arms down is distressed Mary. Between the two, is a flat, darkly-sweet purple, mildly-alive mass with a slim, circular shape and as tall as Mary. In the upper-right within the framework of the group was a single tear, comfortable in its place. In an art-therapy way, the slightly alive purple mass and tear symbolizes the barrier of sadness standing between Mary and Father John.

A sensitive soul, Father John knows what will be, will be, and bids she and her group goodbye, then leaves to attend his church and Fatherly duties.

A welcoming monologue to the visitors would normally be imparted, but Mary can't find discourse within, so she answers the few questions with a nod of the head or a syllable or two. Nevertheless, the group is up for a good Sunday time and remains astounded by the beauty of the Mission's physical surroundings, the abundance of surprises around each corner: the arcades, and low, hand-hewn entrances, the simple wooden baptistery chairs, the nave, the lectern, Jesus on the Cross, the interior courtyard and small, ancient rooms for living quarters for the workmen. The children play under and around the bronze horse and rider, climb around the fountain, skip along under the arch-covered walkways and tussle in the grass.

Parents quietly talk among themselves, watch and love their children playing, enthuse over the history that saturates the surroundings and have a wonderful tour-time. When finished, each comes up to Mary and tells her how much they have enjoyed themselves and enthuse about their experience until, children gathered, they make their way to the parking lot and home.

The visitors didn't expect the spoken part of the tour and didn't miss it. They intended to enjoy themselves and were not deprived of a good Sunday time. Did Mary resolve her problem? Did Father John help her or discuss her difficulty with her? Is there an end to the John and Mary story? I guess the answer is no, but I love them all and I love you all.

Soul - Gary Zukav

I'm reading Gary Zukav's book called, *The Seat of the Soul*. I have to keep in mind his theories are his theories. If *he* believes what he has written then I assume it is the truth and believe he believes it is the truth. Therefore, what Gary says he believes is also what he says he knows and a major part of who he is! Therefore, he stands for whatever he writes, because that is what he believes, and is a confession about who he is.

You might ask, *"What does he write?"* Well, I've only read 53 pages, so I can't give you a complete report, but so far, he divides people's lives into two parts. The first is what he calls *personality,* and the second is called the *soul.*

Personality seems to be external things that continue through life, such as love, hate, anger, revenge, politics, law enforcement, wars, police, etc. Soul has to do with feelings like reverence for the planet, like knowing and loving the miracle of life, plants, animals, fish, birds, people and the wonder of the Great Forces of Nature.

I have a different view, but think I understand what Zukav is trying to say. Below is another view contrasting to his.

Another view

No one knows where the *"Self"* came from. Without permission, every living *"Self,"* including our universe, appeared from a source called, *"we do not know."* Given us being here, we see the world is packed with Good, only as compared to Bad. Like Yes and No. Good does not exist without its Bad. Yes does not exist without No.

The *"Self"* was born with needs like hunger, thirst, exercise, sex and continuing the species. For that, humans had to work in various environments to get food. Early man had to hunt and raise animals, grow vegetables and fruit, and have a place to live within a tribe to defend his family. To do these things, he had to take an approach requiring a left brain to solve practical problems. I see that is what Zukav calls the *Personality.*

But the human also contains the more primitive Right brain, having feelings like reverence for the planet, loving the miracle of life or Wonder of the Great Forces of Nature, sadness, elation, laughter, gentleness, love for a spouse and family, etc. Zukav says these right brain feeling items are called the Soul, where I like to think the Self contains both the practical and feeling sensations of the Left brain and Right brain, and consider the soul hidden in an area I'd like to call the *"Other,"* located in the *"we do not know"* area.

Fingertip Dream

Immediate scene 1
I'm hanging on by the tips of my fingernails to a colorful balloon that's striped like our beach umbrellas. It's big and bloated and full of air, ready to take off. It's fairly small for a balloon, but certainly large enough to carry a man, me, high into the air, where, if I lost my grasp, I'd fall to the ground and die.

Only my fingertips grasp the tiny ridge upon which I hang and I can't get a good hold with only four fingers, but with the full strength of my arms and a desperate dedication, I'm slowly lifted and tempted to hang on even though I'm undecided whether the trip into the air could be an adventure or a disaster. Slowly, I rise, but too quickly I realize I've not a strong enough hold and will not be able to support my weight, and should I wait a second or two longer I'd surely fall.

The place of the balloon and it's ambivalent partner, me, is over a motor court with a garage next to it. Running horizontally and perpendicular to the garage is a concrete deck with railing to protect someone from falling off or entering, perhaps as I might, from a balloon.

I think I can will myself higher or lower by human instinct or special powers and maneuver the balloon in such a manner that I'm able to glide over the railing and come to rest on the concrete deck.

Seemingly arbitrary and immediate scene 2:
The balloon and I are hovering close over a deck that now surrounds a pool. I misjudge something, lose my hold on the balloon, and pitch backwards and fall into the water. The water is not clear, but a cool green color, and though I'm somewhat pleased to be cooled, I know the filtering system has not been operating for some time and the water might be polluted. I get

out of the side of the pool next to large sliding glass doors on the side of a of a house and see two women peacefully talking. Though I do not know them, I decide to enter through the sliding glass doors and speak to them.

 I slide the door open and enter. I have on muddy, wet gym shoes and the carpet and floor to which I've quietly and gently entered becomes also muddy and wet along the glass and handles of two adjacent sliding glass doors.

 I know that if I step on the dry carpet I will spread mud and water, and being mindful, do not do so. I should be embarrassed if I soiled their carpet, but the women are no longer there and I awake.

Meaning

Last night Marge and I saw "Cow-belles" where a fully clothed, nasty young woman fell into a pool. Yesterday Amanda informed me she needed an unexpected amount of money. My feelings about artwork, and financial considerations and my retirement life with Marge were probably the partially unresolved internal pictures upon which the dream was based.

I Sing My Own Song & Other Things

I know the way to play football. It came with a sandlot invitation to play in the vacant property behind our house in Chicago. It was Saturday morning; there were four on a side, I was eight years old and played in the line. I ran after the opposing backfield man; he was mine and I made him eat dirt. A short while later, one of the opposing team members said, "put two guys on him," which they did, but I scrambled around the luckless blockers and nailed the ball carrier anyway. The day was damp, older kids were on my back, but I was champion. I didn't care who won.

It seemed just a little later, I was nine and we were in La Porte, Indiana. I decided to go out for football, got my uniform and went out and practiced. In the first game of the season I played second string behind another right halfback. When I made it into the game during the last quarter, I remember dropping a ball in the end zone and the crowd yelling, "OOooooh!" Unfortunately, after my first game, my season was over. We moved back to Chicago.

Back in Chicago on Kedzie Avenue, in the seventh grade for a year, I played baseball and became home run champion of the Humboldt Park Boys' Club. Then, several weeks before Austin High School started, I went out for football training. I was large for my age; I loved the game, didn't miss practices, and because it was my first semester in high school, I *wasn't* allowed to play in the scheduled freshman-sophomore games.

In my sophomore year at thirteen, I played fullback and was captain of the fresh-sophomore team, but we either tied or went scoreless and didn't win or lose any games. The season ended, but I do remember the coach physically demonstrating how to tackle. A big, former football player without a uniform, ran at a student and with wildly balding and blowing red hair, rolled in the dust making the perfect tackle and showed us how it was done. I had a superb time hurling myself against tacklers and breaking a few runs. I also punted and kicked extra points. In my third high school year, I played directly behind Bob Phillips who later played in the Marines behind the famous backfield man, Elroy "Crazylegs" Hirsch. That year we had Rocco Carbone, a drop-kicker, as our fill-in fullback. Later, I wrote him a letter when he was in the service in Korea, while I became Austin's chief punter and right halfback for four seasons running. In the army, Rocco was killed in Korea.

Still sixteen in my senior year, I started the first game at right halfback, but from the second game on, I played second string and after four long years, finished up as a second string right halfback. Bob Schneider played the last season in my position. I had a bad knee, an injured neck, and couldn't hit the line hard. Bob did his job beautifully. Dick Kreml and Bill Moore were the center and fullback and co-captains. Joe Lapetina played quarterback, Jim Baer and Herm Kranz played left halfback, and Bob and I played right halfback. Austin High won all eight team games, tied the last one and lost the toss to Tilden, who went on to win the Chicago High School Championship.

I loved football with a passion and it was that sport that dominated most of my high school life. I earned two high school football letters and finished high school football a month before I was seventeen. During high school, I also won three letters in swimming and was co-captain my senior year with my old buddy, George O'Hare. I also won two letters in track by tying for thirds in the City Meets in the pole vault and running the 100 and 220-yard sprints and the initial leg of the 400-yard, 4-man sprint relay. I had a total of seven letters at graduation, the most won by a single individual for the four-year period from 1941 to 1945. My closest competitor was Jim Baer who won five.

At Illinois during my third year in Architecture School, I was a leader in the 28-person independent house intramural sports program. My one-man department handled the teams for baseball, bowling, tennis, track, swimming and touch football. On the two baseball teams, I was the underhand pitcher of the 12"-diameter softball team that did quite well. On the football team, I was quarterback, calling all the plays, throwing all the passes, kicking all the punts and extra points and also playing guard in the line on defense. Our team got to the finals. We didn't win our final game in bowling against the 75-80 person fraternities, but despite the heavy competition, our Independent House came in second, beating almost the entire group of fraternities at the University of Illinois in Champagne-Urbana. When our trophy for all the sports came in, the guys wrapped it up and gave it to me.

Other Things

There were other sports that filled my high school life. When I tried yellow, natural bamboo pole vaulting in high school, I could do it right away because I'd tried it earlier when I was eight years old in Chicago. In the two fresh-sophomore City meets I practiced and went to the finals. Each time, Jim Baer and I tied for third. When I was 13, I loved pole vaulting, and in the practice and meets, ran fast and dug that pole into the hole and leapt for the sky. It may have been a substitute for sex. Unfortunately, I never improved because I didn't get bigger and we had no coaching.

I ran races in high school track. I loved the 40, 100 and 200-yard races. We used to run one after the other. I also loved the running long jump that I also competed in each season. I ran one 200-yard sprint against the future world champion in the 100 and 200-yard sprints named Buddy Young. My cousin said, "at the end, I was "gainin' on 'em", but I suspect Buddy was slowing down.

I swam for three years in high school races, too. I placed first on the team in my events early in my first year, in the 50 and 100-yard races. I would swim the 50, then the 100, and then anchor the four-man, and later, the three-man relays. When I was a senior, in the Chicago city high school championships, I was able to place 3rd in the 50 and 100-yard events and I anchored the three-man and four-man relay teams to a first. I won three letters in the three years I swam.

When first beginning high school as a Fresh-Soph swimmer during the time trials, I beat the nearest contender in the 50-yard freestyle by over a second, then couldn't make the finals because Mother wouldn't let me swim because I had the flu. It bothers me to this day. Later, I placed third in the 50 and 100-meter events in two Chicago City Park Meets during the summer, and fooled around doing 1-1/2's and full gainers on worn city swimming pool park diving boards.

I had more letters than anyone in the 7,000-person high school, and I used sports as a dodge to keep my sensual urges under control. During the normal academic year, I gradually increased my grades, and by the year 1944 had all S's, the highest grades possible at Austin High School, and joined the National Honor Society. During the school year, the class I most remember was my architecture class, taught by Mr. Jarvis. I was in his class for three years. The class was held in a spacious corner room with large glass windows on two sides. Mr. Jarvis would have his class practice lettering, or delineating Greek and Roman columns in special black inks. His classes met daily for two or three hours, and I used to sigh with relief when I attended to do my architectural work. Later, because of my three-year major, I was able to skip the first semester of design work at the University of Illinois.

The Austin High School buildings on Central Avenue were large enough for 7,000 students. It had long, four-story hallways with rooms on each side, and a wide yard with small trees between the newer four-story brick structure and the smaller three-story building. The old building had a large gym with a loft-hung track for distance runners to practice, and in the underground hallway below the campus and between the two buildings, we used to run 40-yard sprints. Jim Baer and I used to work out on the vault in the smaller building's gym. The 40-yard pool was also underground. The gym for basketball was bigger and better. The grounds for marching the band were outside as were the local snack bars and restaurants.

I was in numerous school papers due to my athletic ability, and it subsequently led to being elected Austin High School student Senior Class President. The short Giving and Receiving gift speech before well over 1,000 people in the Austin High School Auditorium *(with loft)* was one of the most difficult times of my life. I got through it. Then, along about November, during my last year as a member of the National Honor Society, I received an award from Chicago Daily News as the west side's Most Outstanding Student.

Consciousness

1 – No one knows how the universe began.

2 – Through our limited telescopes, scientists have tracked the universe back 13.8 billion years to within a fraction of a second before the universe snapped forward out of somewhere or nowhere to what we see today.

3 – Some scientists say it came into existence from nothing.

4 – Others say it came into existence from an unknown field of some kind; electrical or other active or gaseous material.

5 – No one knows or can show, or even theorize how the Universe came into being.

6 – From a common sense standpoint, things don't spring from nothing to any size, particularly to a size as big as the universe.

7 – And so the unanswered question sits on the fence like a bird, and we wonder when it's going to lay the egg.

Time is So Long, Humans Don't Get It.

1 – Our planet is unique and we haven't discovered any planet like it, though we believe many are out there, but they're impossible to get to because they're too far away. *(A person is like a planet, there's only one and no choice to leave.)*

2 – On this planet we have another of its miracles, *a living human being.*

3 – In the beginning, living things on earth weren't here. Then, through no request of their own, living things found themselves here. Then, after a short period of time, they died *(an extinction)* and joined the ongoing eternity. **Not here! Here! Not here!** You might say, why?

4 – How did living things begin? On Earth, we know when they appeared, but we don't know why or how. What's the answer?

Consciousness

5 – If we take it for granted, OK! We don't know how, but we're here and I have consciousness!

6 – Certain minds can imagine a powerful force like God imposing consciousness on each of us we call self. Now you see it. Now you don't.

7 – For consciousness to exist, a living being must have self-awareness. You must have a self or there's nothing that can be aware of anything. If there is no self, then there is no possibility of awareness. We are not sure that other living beings are aware enough to identify them as having a self: does a bear, a giraffe, a fish, or a bird know if or why they're here?

8 – If the living being has no idea of who he or she is, the living being falls into a percentage of awareness between not knowing (0%) and knowing (100%).

9 – How does an aware human being form a percentage of awareness even to another human being, let alone another animal, raccoon, polar bear, ant, dolphin, etc.?

10 – One can't, but it's improper to forget the question and let it go at that. Getting closer to the answer takes more information.

11 – Are there degrees of consciousness? What is an example of consciousness?

12 – Example: As a human, I wrote and gave a speech in class and was complemented by my friends; the teacher liked what I said and gave me an "A." Going to sleep that night, I was pleased with myself. I liked my work and took pride that others liked it, too. The good feelings I had were examples of my consciousness of myself.

13 – To write about the speech, I used my brain and five senses, and typed it out on the computer and spoke to the class on what I'd written. That was more attention to detail; one of the forms of consciousness, but not all of consciousness.

14 – Though an amoeba is alive, it hasn't eyesight, ears, nose, mouth, nervous system or brain and probably a minimum

of feeling. To persist, it moves away from things that would destroy it and toward things that would foster it. Thereafter it divides and continues the species.

15 – Does the amoeba have consciousness? Does it have the ability without a brain or nervous system to ruminate when the day is over and take pride in its actions for the day? Can it say, I did that or shouldn't have done that? Who will be the listener?

16 – Without four of our five senses, or my dad's type of reasoning, I'd suggest it does not!

17 – You might tell me neither of us knows. There are so many things *(see above)* in the Universe totally devoid of common sense; the amoeba may have another kind of consciousness unaware to us.

18 – To ask a question, what is the percentage in anyone's mind that an amoeba has an awareness of some kind, a sense of self, an overall perspective of itself in the world or a similar consciousness, or even another kind of consciousness than ours?

19 – I might answer, "Miniscule." But since I can't be an amoeba as well, I can't know for sure. Not knowing is like the impossibility of discovering awareness after death, or knowing what's behind and irrevocably locked door, or what's inside an unopenable box. And so the answer for my Dad and me has to be, *"We don't know!"*

I Owe Life Nothing

If life owes me nothing, that's fine.

Then, I owe life nothing and we're square.

Until now, I have felt I owed life something.

I owed my ex-wife and children something and in many ways, they claimed I owed them something.

My ex-wife still claims I owe her something, though I believe our marital settlement to be more than fair.

Since my family was synonymous with my life, I felt I owed life something.

I find now, life owes me nothing.

My ex-wife claims she owes me nothing.

I cannot look to my children for payment, nor do I want it from them.

Since those I love and the life I love owe me nothing, I declare I owe life nothing and we are square and we can go our separate ways.

I See the World This Way

The **Religion of Common Sense** must encompass the whole universe and especially our entire world, since our one planet *(off of which, we shall not get)* is the mother of all life and all living creations, animal and mineral. They are Earth's siblings and demand to be treated as such. So, I see the world this way: Between Venus and Mars, Earth swirls around the sun, while at the same time, rotates around itself at the rate of about 1,000 miles an hour. This rapid, twirling movement of our planet, made up of about 70% water and 30% land energizes the atmosphere, causing winds, rains, tornadoes, hurricanes, fog and dust storms. The Earth, a metal-based planet *(as opposed to a gas-based planet like Saturn, Jupiter or Uranus)*, is halfway through its nine-billion-year existence. It has a molten core of lead boiling away at its center that regularly spouts volcanoes, spewing tons of carbon dioxide and life-enhancing minerals into the atmosphere. If a volcano spews forth beneath the ocean, it may precipitate a tsunami, causing huge waves that devastate shorelines. The perpetual rotation also forces powerful ocean currents to curl and twist in changing patterns around projecting islands and landforms.

Our life-giving protection is made of an extremely thin layer of atmosphere compared to the size of the earth. It consists of 78% nitrogen and 21% oxygen. The habitable space for all living things is well below that of the world's highest mountain at 29,032 feet. Twelve thousand feet above sea level is the highest most anyone might safely travel without eventually blacking out. Average timberlines are 10,000 feet below the highest mountains. Life, foliage, fish, mammals, reptiles and insects, including everything that lives, is compelled and forced to adapt to these un-asked for, but persistent and continuing facts and forces. We are truly the offspring of Earth, our miraculous Mother. Seen from space, this tiny, brilliant, watery-blue ball with its large, white, circling moon is alone, lost and singular in the surrounding black vastness of space, and we're on it in the dark of the universe. We can't get off! We're in this miraculous terrarium until we die, and our bones will remain for over four-and-a-half billion years until the heat of a dying sun swallows the planet itself. Doesn't that blow your mind?

How Did You Get Into Reflection Photography?

Well, you see, it's like this. I've had a career as an architect doing houses and remodeling in Malibu for over 50 years. Though partially retired, architectural work can be called my day job, giving me time to outlay tremendous sums of money to frame my photographic art and write my plentiful books.

Many years ago, I visited my good friend and structural engineer, Dimitry Vergun, who at that time had his four-person structural engineering studio at 17th and California Street in Santa Monica. It was a routine visit about my newly-ordered structural work, and I left his office pleased and feeling good having distributed my work to Dimitri, the following professional. Getting to the engineering stage on any job is kind of a milestone, and afterward, having passed the bulk of my job to others, I felt a joyous sense of freedom. I had my camera with me that afternoon and decided to walk, jaunty-jolly, in the Santa Monica Mall; perhaps, take a few pictures.

I parked on top of the parking structure, locked the car, turned around, and was immediately taken by a striking panoramic view of the tops of Santa Monica's beautiful buildings. Naturally, I took a picture. Then, winding down the long stairway on badly worn concrete steps, I exited on a typical Santa Monica alleyway and naturally had to record that as well. I tried to use my compositional skills such as they were, to take especially artistic shots of the backs of professional buildings.

A block or so later, I found myself on the crowded mall with innumerable people of every age and description who waited for lights, or walked happily along, or strolled, or sat on benches, or gathered around tables under yellow umbrellas to have coffee and a little afternoon conversation and dessert. Some were window shopping and others gathered to watch or listen to ever-present public entertainers and street musicians,

How Did You Get Into Reflection Photography? 75

all among wide concrete walkways with audaciously blooming Jacaranda trees and trimmed bushes in the shape of dinosaurs.

I had a photographic field day with a plethora of inanimate subjects and multitudes of people. Besides rather surreptitiously trying to shoot crowds waiting for a stoplight, or taking candid shots of interesting people looking in store windows, or trying to photograph a couple hurrying toward the camera, I found it less embarrassing to photograph those accidental passersby as reflections in store windows. They wouldn't be staring into the lens of my camera and I could be seen as a well-meaning, more cordial fellow. Were I to aim the camera toward them, I could visualize them ripping my camera off my shoulder, and summoning the police, or giving me threatening looks, perhaps, before a boyfriend knocked my block off.

Be that as it may, I'd wait for certain people to come along and photograph their reflection in the plate glass. For a while, this was an obvious success. But later, I couldn't help noticing other reflections in plate glass storefronts. Buildings on the other side of the mall were sometimes brilliantly reflected, and this in combination with whatever else I was shooting beyond the glass was frequently delightfully pronounced and exceedingly beautiful. Then, too, what was behind the glass was often interesting

Then I discovered manikins. They were perfect photographic models. Manikins didn't move. Their expressions were fixed forever. I could move around them, bend low or stand on tiptoes and shoot them from almost every different angle. I said to myself, *"What a find!"* as if no one else had discovered manikins didn't move.

Then I noticed that sometimes the reflections of a lamppost, sign, person, tree limbs or a clipped bush in the shape of a dinosaur was reflected in, let's say, within a manikin's dark blouse. It made an interesting shot. I began to see things differently. Then I saw more reflections in the glass with interesting things behind the glass. The combination of the two was sometimes good and certainly made me the viewer ask questions. What's it all about? How did I get that? Does that mean anything? This shot is weird!

Then it came to me; why not make a book of pictures telling the story of a typical day at the Santa Monica Mall? For the beginning, I'd take my pictures from the top of the parking structure, then add the photos of my descent and into the alleyway, kind of approaching the day. Then photos of the multitudes waiting for the light to change for crossing and the myriad of humanity in every walk of life walking, strolling, sitting or listening on the mall. Then add my newfound interest in strange reflections, which, in some cases, turned into indecipherable abstracts. I thought I'd complete the book by reenactment of the beginning – a return to the car – and making some kind of completion of the day. Returning, I then took more pictures, similar, but different from the first.

When I got home, I downloaded 150 digital images into a file called *original*. After reviewing all the pictures the next day, I rejected about 50 and placed about 100 into a file called *keepable* and began, one by one, cropping and editing pictures, first, from the top of the parking structure, then out into the crowds, the experience on the mall, the initial discovery of the reflection and abstract photos and the return to the car. When I'd finished, I printed a cover with a picture of people called **Santa Monica Mall**, wrote a short Foreword and Acknowledgements, stuck in a personal history with my picture and printed each of the images on my HP Color Printer. It would be cut at six inches by nine inches, spiral bound at Kinko's, and ***Voila!*** A color book called **Santa Monica Mall.**

I didn't reproduce it and sell it. I kept it around the house. I guess I did it for me. I showed it to my wife and to several of our seven kids. Marge's visiting sister from the State of Maine, saw it, and said, along with family and friends, **"OOOH!** and ***AAAAAH!***

and that was my initial sojourn into **Reflection Photography.**

But that's not the end of the story. My stepdaughter, Marge's eldest, who had graduated in photography from Art Center in Glendale, saw the book and was intrigued by my approach. She picked a few of mine as her favorites and commented, *"People who'd made it in the art field needed a 'Schtick." (Since my spell-check hasn't objected, evidently I've spelled* **"schtick"** *correctly. I think it means a method that hasn't been or has not frequently been used before.)* Perhaps reflection photos were my *"schtick!"*

Talking it over with Marge, I became enthused to try another location. I would shoot reflection photos in the promenade at Ventura Harbor. There were good glass windscreens there, with lots of strange reflections. On our next beach trip, in a state of enthusiasm, I took pictures for about an hour and was encouraged by the shots I was evidently getting. When I got home, I took the raw material and began working with it again. I began to see the variety inherent in reflection photos: people out of scale with reflected other people; strange patterns superimposed over a simple white wall; the appearance of a sky totally out of place, etc. In the past I'd always blocked reflections because they were in the way of what I was trying to see through the glass. Now I was accepting them as part of another reality. What I saw plus reflections! I was capitalizing on the better of two worlds, what was behind the glass superimposed with that in front. How was that for a **"schtick!"**?

I was learning reflections add complexity, mystery and delight in seeing more than a photo of an object directly in front. Looking and finding good reflections was surprising and I was astounded at the results. I took advantage of downtown Salinas, California next.

Such was my introduction to photography with reflections.

Art, I Think!

Yesterday, I picked up six of my photographic art pieces at SCIART *(Studio Channel Islands Art Center and Gallery)* in Camarillo. I dropped my keys in the trunk and put in three art pieces and closed the lid. My car dutifully beeped, happily telling me the entire car was securely locked, totally inoperable and things inside were utterly impossible to steal. Panic hit me! I glanced through the back window to see if my worst fears had come true. They were confirmed! I'd locked the car keys inside the trunk!

Disconcerted, I walked back to the gallery and through the front door where the Art Director, Karin Geiger, was advising with an apparently new gallery sitter on her duties for the day. I asked if I could use their land line to call the Auto Club, which they so gracefully did, and told the agent of my problem, gave the gallery address and phone number, and within minutes I got a phone call saying Eddie's Service Man was outside next to my car. Within fifteen minutes of locking my keys in the trunk, I found myself thanking Eddie's Service Man and leaning over the hood and signing the Auto Club paper and realizing I was back in business.

Karin Geiger had left when I returned to SCIART for my other three photos, which I'd laid in a row and left out on the low, 3' x 6' bench-table. I introduced myself to Sylvia, the new gallery sitter, and since no one was about anyway, we started a conversation most artists love; it was about Sylvia's artwork. Among the 30, mostly abstract artworks in the small but delightful gallery, she showed me two of her beautiful encaustic artworks, each about 16" x 36", one vertical and one horizontal.

I told her I'd seen her works at the reception on the Saturday before and thought them marvelous. I complemented her on her Honorable Mention and told her I loved her rendition of the sea powerfully marching across the page and an equally amazing yellow band of clouds and sky sailing along as a bright, attentive friend. In the left/center was a 3"-square wooden box projecting an inch forward of the picture-plane and inside vividly displaying a preserved sea anemone shell. *(I could have bought the artwork just for the omnipotent power of the roiling sea and sky, but the anemone sculpture was a fantastic plus.)*

Asking her to talk more about her work, which is something I love to do with all artists, she replied she loved the cosmos and our moon and planet, the elemental forces of nature, the earth, sky, mountains, water, air and clouds, and wanted to portray her caring for their existence within the contents of the shows theme, which was called *"Cross-Pollination."* Artists were to use two methods of doing one piece of artwork; that is, combine two mediums to see if a new and desirable result would miraculously take place. Sylvia's artwork was, of course, done in two mediums, the background of sea and sky of encaustic, and the box and sea anemone shell, a three-dimensional form, was part of the sculptural medium.

Regarding her love for elemental forces, I told her she sounded just like my wife and best friend, Marge, who did artworks in Prismacolor pencil on paper. In Marge's drawings of especially eroded rocks with magical shapes and shadow patterns descending deeply beneath the ocean's shadowy surface, were shown gently disappearing as if swallowed by water. Her amazing blue and white renditions of clouds sailing through the sky were also examples of her love for the fundamentals of the planet, earth, sky, clouds and water. Sylvia said that during one substantial period of her life, she also loved doing pencil work. I replied with words to the effect of, *"Wow! I can see you have been an artist for a very long time, perhaps all your life!"* She admitted she had and told me she had been one of the first in a community of artists occupying the former mental health facilities at what is now the California State University

Channel Islands. For most of her life, she used to live and work in Camarillo, but now she and her husband had moved south to La Quinta, near Palm Springs.

(I thought to myself, here I am standing before a bona fide lifetime teacher and artist who has expressed herself in a multitude of mediums for perhaps 50 years. Since I have only been showing about two years, I was astounded that a novice like me could show my own work in the company of such a talented, dedicated and professional artist.)

Soon, a second 64-year-old or so artist breezed through the open door. She announced herself as Gwenolyn. Sylvia asked if she were sometimes called *"Gwen."* She quite definitely said, *"No!"* and that she *"only answered to Gwenolyn."* Gwenolyn was who she was and I felt she expressed a silent admonition that hereafter she'd better be called *Gwenolyn*, or else!

I asked Gwenolyn if she had a piece of artwork to pick up. She said yes. Sylvia and I were invited to see an inlaid tile piece still on the wall. It was about 16" wide and about 42" high, depicting dark-brown structural members on each side, while the foreground had a light-colored element of yellowish buildings looking through an elongated center. I complemented her on the distance she achieved which I assumed was her obvious intent. She smiled and I could tell she was pleased.

Both women were tall and slim, looking distinguished. Sylvia was, perhaps, 5' 10", and I'd guess about 60 years old, and Gwenolyn even taller, perhaps 5' 11" and I'd guess about 64 years old. They'd both probably raised families and had a few grandchildren. I'm 84 and a mere 5' 6" high, so I had this image of these two tall, smart looking women talking to this little old short guy dressed in Saturday clothes.

Then the attention turned briefly to me. Gwenolyn noticed three of my reflection photos lying on the low, polished wooden table waiting for me to take them to my car and home.

They were not my best work. In fact I'd given them as free

donations to a SCIART fundraiser where, for $100, the donors got to have dinner, see the art show, listen to an appreciative talk on art and take home an artist member's original piece. The artists, of course, got nothing and the attending art lovers might even have had to buy the artist's work, probably for substantially less than what it was worth, the gallery making the profit. I don't know. I wasn't there. I was just donating my lesser work free for a fundraiser as an altruistic effort to keep art in the public eye.

Gwenolyn thought my work interesting and said she could see I liked color. I explained I liked to do reflection photos and tried to explain what that was. I said, *"I like to shoot pictures through plate glass windows to capture whatever fascinating item was behind the glass in heavily occupied places like Old Town Ventura, or the Thousand Oaks Mall, or Channel Islands Harbor Village, and get not only portions of what was behind the glass, but also whatever was reflected in the glass. In the past I'd always tried to block reflections, but now allowed them to work as part the new art piece. In other words, I now looked for reflections and included them in my artwork."*

I said, *"Where you and Sylvia create artwork out of your soul, your desire, your pleasure, and from the bottom of your being in producing something new and different in the world, you are truly creative artists, where I, on the other hand, am fond of saying, 'I don't create art, I discover it!'"*

They both seemed to understand, and I followed with the fact that I'd been an architect in the Malibu area for 54 years, and had done almost 100 houses and an equal number of remodels. I had worked in Long Beach, Brentwood Village, Santa Monica, Santa Barbara, and Kauai and even went to Greece for a small addition. They seemed impressed with my architectural experience, and I think, because they understood my architectural experience takes a lot of visualization and making critical decisions in line, color, mass and proportion. Because of this, I do think I made a better than average impression about my reflective photography.

I wanted to continue our conversation, but time was of the essence. Marge wasn't feeling well at home and it was urgent I return. But what I would have said and what I do believe is that artwork is a powerful method of communication.

(Considering the above short story as a lead-in to the following essay, we're going to leave my recent friends to their daily devices, and now at a much later date return to what I would have imparted to them, had they had time and a burning passion for a discussion on art.)

Essay on Art

When I see a picture on the wall, it's an attempt by the artist to tell me something. Or, perhaps, better than that, the picture may be trying to tell the artist something about him or herself; a truth the artist wants to tell or is compelled to express.

Since sharing and communicating and telling stories and giving a point of view is a universal human trait, something left over from the Pleistocene Age, it is also archetypal and innate as part of the collective unconscious. There is a willingness and sometimes a compulsion to share our story, whether it's in art, music, writing or invention. That's how it is and that makes me glad. These ideas, stories, viewpoints or willingness to say our piece happen in poetry, music, painting, architecture, sculpture, literature and all forms of creative endeavor, even by the way we dress, treat others and go about our business. Each of us is an individual as different in our DNA as in our fingerprints. We can't hide it, nor should we.

What the picture has to say, I call an agenda. I might say, *"That picture has a clear agenda!"* Or, *"I don't know what this picture means!"* Or, *"I'm in doubt about what this picture has to say."* The dictionary says *an agenda is items of things to be brought up at a meeting.* To me, therefore, within the artwork is contained a group of recognizable objects, shapes, lines, moods, surprises, methods, etc., that are brought to the viewer, hopefully, for better understanding. In other words, viewers are members of the meeting and the picture contains a list, or things to say or be brought forth by the artist for communication and better understanding, hence, an agenda.

An individual piece of artwork will speak differently to everyone who gazes at it, because each viewer will see it from a their own different point of view. The picture has a message. I look for the message or try to feel or reason its *agenda.*

Then, too, I believe art falls into three broad categories:

(1) Art that depicts recognizable objects. *(Non-abstract art)*

(2) Art that depicts no recognizable objects. *(Abstract art)*

(3) Art that depicts both recognizable and non-recognizable objects. *(Combination of non-abstract and abstract art.)*

I must admit I'm a percentage type of person. When I think of thoughts and desires in humans and artwork, I see them in percentages. To me, there is no such thing as black and white. Everything has a gray of some sort. To me, everything is a little tainted by its opposite. This belief gets me off the hook in many situations, for if I say a thing is one way, there is always a chance I'm wrong – even if its just a little. Please cut me a little slack in this essay. That's why the title is "***Art, I Think!***"

(1) Art that depicts recognizable objects.

This category is the easiest grouping to understand because what you see is what you get. If there is a picture of a person in a boat on water, the artist is trying to tell us about persons on boats in water. Of course there may be other things as well: seagulls, flying fish, whales, a squall in the distance. A young boy may be fishing with hills or mountains reflected in the lake, or a blazing sunset with dramatic clouds sweeping over silhouetted mountaintops. It means the artist is trying to tell us about how wonderful it feels to be a young boy fishing at sunset. We can use our cerebral cortex to understand the artwork on a deeper basis; our right brain is attuned to feelings, hunches, color, emotion, loud noises, fear, etc., and the left brain understands logic, history, mathematics and languages, etc. By and large, the bulk of these artworks relates to this category.

(2) Art that depicts no recognizable objects. *(Abstract art)*

How do I react to a picture without something to which I can identify? Recognizing objects will give me a clue, but if there is none, what then? If I can't use my cerebral cortex to say to myself, *"Oh! I recognize that; it's a person, or car, or iceberg, or whatever it is, etc.,"* then I'm in trouble. I haven't a clue to figure out what the artist is trying to tell me. It is easy to be lost as to the picture's agenda. The agenda, if there is one, must be envisaged in another way. If I see a picture of a beautiful girl, the emotions and memories of girls leap into my consciousness, usually so many I can't think of them all. This results in feelings of attraction or knowledge, or both. A beautiful girl may remind me of my wife, or someone I knew in high school, and what she's wearing gives me a stronger feeling for what kind of person she is, or she may remind me of a girlfriend I've lost, or innumerable things to which I can only speculate. For another person, the image might be different, such as, *"my mother used to look like that."* If the girl was at a beach on a sunny day, I might think, *"Boy! I wish I knew that girl on the beach!"*

But, in art where there are *no* recognizable objects, thoughts or judgments are more likely to come from the right side or intuitive side of the brain. I might use my instinct to decide, *"Do I like this? Is this good? What does this artwork mean? What's its agenda? I've never seen something like this before. Am I delighted? Am I revolted? Do I experience any particular mood? How do I categorize this picture?"* With recognizable objects, I am led into thinking about the meaning of the picture from the recognizable objects within the picture. The objects, or combination of recognizable objects, are something I can hang on to regarding my feelings or knowledge about the artwork. But this new, abstract artwork is without the necessary clues! Clearly, the intuitive side of the brain must be used.

Abstract art seems to fall into two broad categories: abstract art that has something to say *(an agenda),* and abstract art that is just beauty for beauty's sake; pleasing colors and shapes to look at. Abstract art with *an agenda* may involve a picture showing motion, speed, power, drifting, etc., or any poetic word or poetic combination of words of which you might think.

Some abstract pictures may seem related to music. Musical critics are proficient at describing music. There is a wonderful scherzo near the end of Beethoven's Ninth Symphony that has such color and power and force and willingness to persist, it's impossible to explain in words. It can only be felt through the medium of music. After the Los Angeles Symphonic Orchestra played Beethoven's Ninth, in effect an L. A. Times Review said,

"The opening movement had a stern strength, an order to listeners of intent... The scherzo was tight, tense, and vivacious... If the symphony was the world in microcosm, this was adolescent life force, with sweetening and deepening lyrical melodies in the return."

Beethoven's talent and sensibility to course beyond human barriers is sometimes termed "Godlike." Abstract artwork can speak to us in this same non-verbal, Godlike way; tight, tense, vivacious, adolescent life force, sweetening, deepening lyrical melodies, etc. Good abstract non-recognizable art can speak to us from the most inner, poetic parts of our soul – or not.

In viewing non-recognizable art, the left side of the cerebral cortex may not seem involved. When attending an abstract art showing, what I personally feel may be, do I like it or not? Or remembering I'm a percentage man, do I like it x% and dislike it y%? *(Yes! No! AAAeee!)* I soon discover I'm using feelings on the right side of my cerebral cortex; the more primary part of the brain originally developed when humans similar to those present came on our planet. The right side of the brain was the one that developed prior to the left side of the brain, which later allowed us to remember and record the past and speculate on the future. An abstract picture requires I *not* use my left brain or intelligence and I *do* use my right brain or instinct.

How is this achieved? One way, of course, is by line, color, mass, direction, lightness, darkness, etc., or anything that might be reminiscent, or strong and sensitive enough to produce an *"I like"* feeling, or an *"I dislike"* feeling, or anything in between.

Let's say a fellow artist makes an excellent piece of abstract art. How do I know it's excellent? Because I am me and it is I who think so! *(So it is for you. This attitude is free to keep.)* The work's a diptych – two, 24"-square mixed media paintings placed side by side, 1/4" apart. Marge asked what they looked like. I said, *"Well, there were two 24"-square paintings on canvas, both yellow/tan in color, portions of which had a sand texture and portions of which had a smooth/plane texture. Three-dimensional, gauze-like forms moved in and out, sometimes disappearing and sometimes emerging through the paint. Each side of the diptych had what looked like fat lines cutting edge-to-edge across the artwork horizontally, and crossing edge-to-edge vertically. The color and designs of each section, though not the same, were compatible, and I thought the two paintings worked well together."* Get the picture? No? The above long sentence proves it's hard to describe an abstract artwork verbally. I knew this! I just wanted to make you and Marge thoroughly understand I can't describe a painting with words. Pictures and writing are two different methods of communication.

But, if there was one, what feeling did I get from the diptych? I suppose I understood the colors of the two works were compatible, unified, and well-thought out. The thoroughness of the execution allowed me to know the seriousness of the artist whose attention to detail left nothing to chance. The crosses and colors and textures were reminiscent of the desert and the yellow color made me feel intelligence and the sun. On the whole, the work is sunny, optimistic, warm, evocative of the desert, smart and blatantly clear.

Did I like it or not? Yeah! I sort of liked it! But, compared to what? I'd presume to every other abstract work I've ever seen in my whole life, but is it fair to compare a friend's work in a local gallery to every other abstract work I've ever seen in my whole life? Of course not! But we're not talking fair, are we? Was it the best I've seen in the past three months of this year? Probably not! Do I know what the artist had in mind when he painted the work? No, but it definitely had sunny and hot desert overtones, but I'd love to know if the artist had a different idea. If I did, that would add depth to my understanding. I know he'd give me a new perspective and if I read the painting correctly, might even confirm my own viewpoint. If I understood what the painter was trying to tell me wouldn't I then have more knowledge? Isn't knowledge more important than lack of knowledge? Isn't knowledge power? Wouldn't I have more power?

(3) Art that depicts both recognizable and non-recognizable objects. *(Combination of non-abstract and abstract art.)*

In some art, both recognizable objects and non-recognizable objects are used in combination to achieve whatever the artist is trying to say. The use of this combination can be in many different proportions: half recognizable, half non-recognizable, one-third recognizable and two-thirds non-recognizable, or the reverse, or any conceivable relationship of proportions. I'm assuming you are also a *"percentage"* kind of a person, and you get the idea. At this moment, I must say this is the category I like best. Why? Because it is necessary to use both sides of the brain. (a) what do the recognizable objects tell me? If it's a puppy, I am told puppy stories, if there's a bird, I'm told bird stories, if there's a person, I'm told person stories, etc. (b) What kind of feelings do I get from the abstract qualities of motion, calmness, chaos, order, musicality, humor, disgust, dignity, and the myriad of related emotions and connotations contained in the picture? I like a picture with mystery or humor, or one with qualities that speak to me on a level other than simple, straightforward knowledge that requires nothing except being awake and alert. I like *surprise* in seeing, passion in execution and questions upon observation.

I've heard it said some artists put their work on view and leave it to others, if anything occurs to them at all, to get what they can. They want to expose whatever individual perspective the viewer has to offer in combination with their own work for the total experience. In effect, the artist says, *"It's there! It's yours! Get what you can! Use whatever brainwork and feelings you possess and that's the answer."* Then, I might ask, who brings the most, the artist or the viewer? If an artist chooses not to discuss his work, that's his choice and I don't fault him. If he chooses to discuss his work, I for one would be interested to know how he came to create that particular picture. Some artists choose not to communicate verbally, but only through their artwork and that's OK! Many musicians communicate only by composing and playing music and that's OK. Perhaps what artists and musicians are trying to say can't be told in any other way than by their particular medium. They shouldn't be forced to verbally explain themselves. The music or artwork speaks for them. Nor do I demand a sculptor or photographer or musician be verbal. Being an architect, the architect *must* be verbal if only to explain his designs and excite his clients, but are artists different animals? I've sometimes thought I would really like to know what was in the artist's mind when he came up with his or her particular work. What the artist tells me and how he or she tells me would clarify and give dimension to what the artist has created. The artist would give me the artist's viewpoint while allowing me to have mine, thereby opening an interesting discussion about what the artist and I both see and know. Knowledge between us would then be exchanged and we'd both grow. Is it not true that *"Knowledge is Power!"*

All this brings me to the subject of the *meaning* of art. Of course all art has meaning of some sort, but one idea is *no meaning at all.* If I ask an artist what he or she is trying to express? The artist might answer, I don't know! Meaning the artist had no idea about what he or she expressed. Nevertheless, it was he or she that turned out the art and not me or anyone else, therefore, he or she has shown us a part of the artist that perhaps even the artist doesn't know about him or herself. Or maybe if the artist were less than positive about the final work, the artist might tell himself or herself, *"Someone else may like this work even if I don't, so I think I'll send it up the pole and see if anyone salutes."* There are as many points of view on "meanings" as there are in life on all artworks. I think I know my own version of meaning. How? They're surprising! They're different! They're a good idea! They evoke emotion. They ask questions. They provoke thought. Or, I instinctually love them even if I'm not sure why! Somehow when I love my work, I love myself. I guess that's saying I'm doing art so I can love myself. Marge, my wife, demands her work *sing* before it's completed. She says, *"It's not done 'til it sings!"* For me, a good work must have mystery and in some way be unusual. It must communicate a unique point of view. A new work, a new point of view, a new piece of artwork is something only the artist can do. A good artist must have a healthy ego. He or she not only has to think of a great idea, but also has to put it out there for everybody to see. If he or she does, his or her artwork has *meaning!*

In general, what does any artwork have that has *meaning?* Artwork is always subjective. A work may have meaning to person A, but not to person B. What one viewer takes from the picture, a lot, some, or very little, is different for another. What one artist communicates in his pictures is also different for every artist, as are levels of the artist's expertise. They are all different for both viewer and artist, and the huge number of artists accounts for the horrendous, outstanding, massive, uncountable variety of artworks produced second by second, minute by minute, on every day of the week throughout the years, and sometimes on Sundays, by those who consider themselves working artists and those compelled to be artists. How then, in God's holy grace, can we talk about *meaning* in art? Isn't all art meaningful? Yes! I'll give it that. From the youngest three-year-old to the wobbly, stoop-shouldered centenarian, art is meaningful. And I'd have to include all artists who produce all the art in the world, and they are producing meaningful art – if only to them.

I love all artists, but where does that leave me? No matter their work, don't my opinions count? Aren't I entitled to have my own preferences? A better question to ask my self might be, *"What art is meaningful to me?"* I'm loath to hurt a fellow artist's feelings and it's not my intent to shout negativity at those artists whom I consider friends, but don't I have the right to my own likes and dislikes? I want to discuss and learn from my own praises and criticisms of my own and others' work while hearing the same from all those interested. With the intent of sharing information, then, I'd like to think, verbally, about how and where I stand – sort of like preparing for some future test to be given by the public.

Considering all kinds of art, what occurs to me first is *thoughts*. All humans have *thoughts* from the left brain and right brain. People usually use both, though I'd submit artists tend to be more right-brained than left. Since most people and artists can't help using their whole brain, please agree with me that if the left/right brain theory bothers you, there may be different words meaning the same thing; "reasonable" *(left brain)* or "intuitive" *(right brain),* or being thoughtful, intellectually *(L B)* and instinctually *(R B)*.

The second thing that occurs to me is the word *connotation.* A *connotation* is whatever the word implies or suggests. It is related to *free association.* The word *"sky"* connotes clouds, wind, air, night, stars, sun, moon, sunsets, hurricanes, birds, etc. The phrase "peanut butter" connotes sandwich, jelly, toast, bread, joy of eating with a glass of cool milk, early childhood, what my mother made for me for lunch, etc. Are you with me so far?

In category (1) *Art that depicts recognizable objects,* I would say whatever the recognizable object(s) is or are, they will have *connotations.* As an illustration, if the painting or photograph is of a cuddly brown puppy lolling playfully on a couch with its paws in the air, the story of the artwork is question-free. The connotations are clear: love, warmth, innocence, reminders of childhood, furry softness, etc. The couch might be clean and pure like most of our friends' living rooms, or it could be worn and threadbare, possibly in a poorer neighborhood. Artwork over the couch might be sophisticated; perhaps a painting by Renoir, indicating the puppies' owner has an artistic flare, or a picture of five soldiers raising the flag over Iwo Jima, indicating, perhaps, the residence of a veteran, or a child's artwork Scotch-taped to the wall, a *connotation* indicating hominess and love for children.

The puppy on the couch with the artwork above has no questions. It falls into the category of depicting recognizable objects. All recognizable objects have connotations. Connotations tell me what the picture is about. The story is clear. There is no mystery, but the picture's value lies in the mood it strikes, the relationships of line, form color, proportion, composition, etc., and all the technical things that make a good picture. What if there's a coyote peeking through the crack in the slightly open door? Aha! Something else is happening. But in the photo just expressed, viewers and I understand the message of the artwork and like it or not, we *"get it!"*

Whether the picture is a *meaningful* work of art depends on the subjective view of the observer. If the picture is dark or in bright sunshine with strange, unusual textures of paint, watercolor, oil, pencil, encaustic, serigraph, etc., any one of which, or possibly all may indicate whether it's meaningful or not. It remains undecided until I see it, and only I can decide, if it has an *agenda* and contains *connotations,* and therefore, allows me to enjoy it and, if necessary, ask a few questions.

In category (2), *Art that depicts non-recognizable objects,* if upon first appearance, there is nothing depicted with which to relate, I have to remain uninformed. If there are no violent rainstorms descending on a rocky valley or deer suddenly alert in a darkened forest, there is apparently nothing in the picture that brings anything to mind. There's just color, line, form, shape, composition, mass, proportion, etc. What good is that? Since I don't recognize anything, I guess I'll have to use a different part of my brain. Perhaps *connotations* will be of some use before I can decide whether I like it or not and on the artwork's worth or meaning.

Some abstract artworks are very good. I know that because, evidently, I have used a different part of my brain to understand the new unrecognizable artwork. That part would be the more primitive, intuitive right side of the brain; the instinctual portion just inside my cranium, the feeling part of my cerebral cortex, the gut-level impact of the piece. What else is there? Intelligence is not going to do it, but if I have an intellectual side to the thinking, brainy part of my gray matter, I suppose I might as well use that, too. But the brainy part is not the portion to be used in seeing and judging abstract art. Nevertheless, I feel it's important to use *all* the types of equipment possible if I'm to give it my all. I need to know what it is the abstract artist is trying to tell me. Perhaps it cannot be expressed in words and that's why he or she is using art as his or her means of communication.

It turns out *humans are pattern-making machines.* Even if the artist hasn't intended it, so two round circles will usually be seen as eyes. In the moving clouds I'll see recognizable shapes of sheep, wolves, Abraham Lincoln, a McGoo character, etc. In a geode, I'll find a perfect Jesus Christ on the cross. I'll see recognizable shapes in abstract patterns found in the bark of trees. Why? Because when humans were living in the Pleistocene age, though they could hardly see predators, they had to be aware of how they could be seen so they wouldn't be eaten. Seeing that which would eat you became a survival thing. Humans were trained to see and recognize lions and tigers and bears to survive. If they didn't make out the silent twitching of a tiger's tail or its whiskers or notice its beady yellow eyes quietly flashing out of the darkness, they'd be *eaten!* Children seeing the *Boogie Man* is a left over of the hunter/gatherer age, where humans needed to suddenly notice a ferocious animal that was going to kill them and they know they will *die!*

That's *part* of the reason why *humans are pattern-making machines.* The other part is that the eternal oracle declares, *"All humans are omnivores who eat both vegetables and meat."* Before man was an omnivore, he was a hunter and carnivore. Animals that were man's food – pigs, fowl, rabbits, deer, and yes, even elephants – were suitably disguised and naturally colored and patterned to blend into the natural surroundings, in effect, to disappear. But man's midsized intestine is suitable to digest either animal or vegetable, and so hunt he did.

Since it made no sense to sneak up on a wild raspberry bush or slink into a ripe strawberry patch, when one was hungry, it was smart to have an arrow poised in the bow when detecting an almost invisible deer frozen in place 50 yards away. Man had to make trustworthy patterns in his mind to see and kill live food. He had to see things in the dim light of early dawn or the confusing colors of twilight just before night. Man can't help searching nature for recognizable patterns, and will continue to do so even in our present, modern day. Sometimes certain shapes, colors and sizes will recall patterns of some sort that may have *connotations*. And *connotations* can bring about real feelings of like, dislike, fear, love, misgivings, apathy, resistance, or any poetic word of which you or I can think.

If I try looking at an artwork seeing only yellow, I quickly spot all the yellow portions throughout the work. If I concentrate on seeing only blue, soon I notice all the blues here and there as they occur. The same thing goes for shapes. If I try to notice everything vertical, quickly all the verticals are revealed. The same for diagonals, circles, ovals, hexagons, dodecahedrons and orange peels, including faces, animals, trees, plants, whales and everything that can possibly be imagined. They all are revealed to me because I choose to see them. Be it said, *"... so that a man wants to see, so shall he see."*

Let's get something out of the way. Unless the picture's story is pure chaos and obviously intended otherwise, good artwork must pay attention to harmony. Though I admit sometimes there can be harmony amidst chaos. But then at this time I'm not addressing harmony and chaos. As you and I already know, when expressing harmony, there is a strong relationship between all parts. There is direction toward which the picture moves. Toward color, line, recall, composition, or moods, whether grumpy, silly, apathetic, serious, mysterious, contemplative, light-hearted, etc. Though I'm sure I'll get arguments, I mean to say that in good artwork, the correct use in a correct relationship must apply. Good artwork and in all creative endeavors like good poetry, prose, music, sculpture, architecture, car engines, trains, airplane parts, etc., should be well related, well-composed, well-thought out, well-considered and contain the elements of harmony. Let's hear it for well-related harmony. Because it's so, we can go to Seattle or send men to the moon or create wonderful two or three dimensional works of art.

An old saw, *"A correct piece of artwork is one that can't be added to or subtracted from."* If something could have been left out, it should have been left out. If something could have been added, it should have been added. In a good piece of artwork, there should be exactly enough, but not too much, and I confess, I believe it!

If I'm shown a piece of abstract artwork, I'll do my best to understand what the artist has to say. I'll consider shapes, lines, volumes, color, tension, composition, intent, drawing, direction, dynamics, statics, recall, symmetry, non-symmetry, force, etc. – the whole idea. *(There can be some bad ideas, though I realize that will be only my opinion.)* Note: If the picture is to be professionally done and evocative of feeling, and *(see)* if meaning is to be clear, some or all of these things *must* apply to all three categories.

That said, back to abstract, non-representational art. In considering art with non-recognizable objects, I am forced to use the instinctual portion of my brain. In considering many kinds of abstract art, I've seen some in which the artist seemed to have splashed all kinds of colors and forms and volumes of art all over the place. My first reaction is, *"This art's a mess!"* Whether or not this is so, something will tell me I like or don't like it, but probably *not* my left brain. Afterward, my left brain, my reasonable brain, might say *why* I like the abstract work. The left brain, intellect, is used to justify what the intuitive, right brain experiences. What about color? Colors have *connotations,* too.

When Marge and I first met, we attended an improvisational dance class for 12 years. In one of our classes, rather than learn the tango, waltz or foxtrot, we had to find our own personal movements through dancing under different colored lights that shone from the ceiling. For instance, as an individual within a small group, we found similar movements to all the colors: blue, green, yellow, red, purple, white, etc. When the group of eight danced under green lights, we made slow movements; contemplative, thoughtful and flowing, similar to being underwater. When under blue lights, most everyone was light on their feet, apparently floating in the sky or air, arms moving and raised. Under yellow, the group moved in more thoughtful, studied, optimistic patterns. Under red, which the books say is the most arousing color, dancers strangely became either more violent, powerful, and aggressive or very quiet, submissive and compliant. In dancing red, there was no in-between. Purple brought out pompous, royal movements like a queen in purple robes. Bright white brought out optimism, hopefulness, cheer, confidence, buoyancy and intelligent feeling movements. In the group, white light was by far the happiest, most fulfilling and engrossing of the movements. Since most all of the dancers moved similarly inside each of the various colored lights, I now assume colors have strong and similar connotations of the moods and feelings the dancers expressed.

It is possible to understand more about the *connotations* of colors by automatic writing. Writing automatically (i.e., without much thought, or writing *"unconsciously"*), when I thought of the color *(or non-color)* white, I'd think or write the words "white," "light," *"let there be light,"* "daylight," "sunlight," "moonlight," "enlightened," "seeing," "I like light!", etc. If I were to decide on the color *(or non-color) black*, I might think or write "dark," "unseeing," "pitch black," "go-away colors," "mystery," "unknowing," "unenlightened," etc. If I were to examine the color *red*, I'd think or write the words "rose," "Santa Claus," "blood," "danger," "provocative," "fingernails," "stoplight," etc. If I were to do *blue*, I'd think "sky," "ocean," "calm," "clouds," "waves," "unhappy," *"the blues,"* "common," "eyes," etc. If I were to automatically write about *yellow*, I might think "sunlight," "chickens," "birdie with a yellow bill," "bright," "smart," "sunny," "sandy," "optimistic," "cowardly," etc. If *green*, I might write "sea," "lake," "trees," "bushes," "lawn," "grass," "money," "uninitiated," etc. And so I see there is a relationship – usually a very unconscious relationship – between colors and what's in the viewer's unconscious mind. These *connotations* are dominant in art as well as dance.

Back to art with non-recognizable objects. I assume, therefore, that I respond instinctually to colors according to the different moods as expressed above, and I assume, because I do, everybody does.

Consider lines. Diagonal lines are *dynamic.* They indicate tension, movement, unrest, agitation, direction, etc., while vertical and horizontal lines are *static.* Verticality can be uplifting or descending, raising or lowering the spirits. Horizontal lines or the movement of horizontal lines can be reminiscent of flat plains, the desert, the sea's horizon line and a substantial plane upon which anything can rest at ease and without anxiety. Vertical lines are at rest and powerful and can carry great loads. Horizontal lines are restful portions upon which to build. Diagonal lines, not so! Diagonal lines move on an angle. They are not at rest. Vertical and horizontal lines are comfortable and remain in place. They have no ax to grind. They are dependable. We can trust them. When I see an abstract artwork, the combination of diagonal lines or vertical and horizontal lines give me a *dynamic* feeling or a *static* feeling.

What about curved lines? What are the connotations of a curved line? *Connotations* of a curved line: When I see or think of a curved line, then my automatic thoughts or my unconscious thoughts are the curve of a woman's hips, softness, the mountainous horizon, the arc of the sun, the turning of the world, a curve as the shortest distance, round, cylindrical, oval, French curve, orbit, a thrown rock high, curving to earth, etc. And of course there are multitudinous variations. What about a horizontal line that swoops up? It is horizontal and ends in an upward swirling curve, or a horizontal line ending in a downward swooping curve. What are the *connotations* of up and down? When I write unconsciously of up, I'd use the words "positive," "rising," "dawn," "pulling upward," "raising a fish out of water," "positive," "gaining a foothold," "winning," "good grades," "the best," "heaven," etc. But what is my thinking about the word *down*? I'd use the words "negative," "slipping," "failing," "falling," "hell," "losing," "age," "dropping," etc. So, I can see *dynamic* and *static* and *curved* lines have *unconscious* meanings and give rise to the instinctual or right part of the brain that has to do with *gut feelings.*

Of course, there are concave shapes and convex shapes, aren't there? But concave and convex can only be noted if related to a vertical, straight-line shape. The vertical shape is static, reliable, trustworthy and a shape I can have faith in because it has a history of always delivering. A vertical *(as well as a horizontal shape)* is a benchmark against which other shapes, shall I say, less reliable shapes can be measured. If a concave shape is related to a vertical shape, I see it's concave. If a convex shape is also related, I can tell it's convex. You see, the vertical or horizontal shapes tell me the truth about each and I can tell you which is which. Are other shapes as reliable as a vertical or horizontal shape? Is *reliable* a useful word when talking about art?

In abstract art, I may see patterns of recognizable objects – or not – and those objects have connotations and what I might derive from the connotations by free association will begin to reflect my feeling toward any piece of abstract art.

And what about a few large, easy to understand, well-spaced colored shapes, as against a multitude of unorganized shapes and colors jamming the frames - simple as against complicated? What about harmony, or lack thereof, in the two compositions?

Now I've run out of gas, but you get the point.

Life and Death

In my own *"common sense"* bible I believe when a person dies the person is no more. When I die, my works and I may live on in the memories of others, but as to the flesh and blood reality of myself, and my one-of-kind personality, I'm gone.

Then, considering the cosmos and quantum physics and the history of man and all religions, few of them know about me and can't care because, *"They can't miss what they don't know." (A tenet in my common sense bible.)* A few generations hence, I will no longer exist in the memory and minds of others.

Therefore, it's important to me in this final chapter in my life *(I'm well over 90 years old)* that I know I was here. In fact, I want to record for myself I know I was here and alive with emotions and feelings and knowledge for a lifetime. I'm recording what has been the most important to me, mentioning my birth, early childhood, schooling, marriage, raising children, life work, athletic adventures, two wives and their deaths, retirement, architecture, art and writing.

These are things that *happened* in my life, but I must also mention my experience of life and that involves being aware of the whole of that of which I'm aware. It includes the violent living actions of everything on the Earth; wind blowing leaves, waves breaking like thunder on the beach, the relentless following of light by dark, gentle clouds, mountains, rainstorms, tornadoes, earthquakes, tsunamis, war, peace, laughter, etc.

How You Know You're Here

Ever not notice yourself? Ever shave in the morning and not look at your face? Ever walk downtown, jaunty, jolly, thinking of nothing special, walking thoughtlessly, and mindlessly and just taking the next step? Ever look out from your eyes and never look in? Ever live life, not by going anywhere, or doing anything, just moving forward, step-by-step, like everybody else? **You May Not Be Here!**

If the answer is yes or no, there are ways to verify, but if you're like me, you may never have considered **whether or not you're here.**

Here are a few clues: If you're going on a hike by yourself, let's say, down a dirt pathway that meanders parallel to a little-traveled, two-lane road, and suddenly you have to sneeze and you squint your eyes and snuff up your nose, with hands on knees so weak you're almost falling down, and taking a deep breath, you brace yourself, glance at the sky, and wait interminably, and when you actually sneeze, you lose all consciousness and awareness of yourself ever having anything to do with this planet. Then, it comes, violently, with a humungous ***"Aaah-choo!!"***

When you've come to, and noticed your nose is damp and you wipe it, and wipe that on your running shorts, you can be sure **you are here!**

Or, you're walking on the beach where waves have just broken on the sand, and you're thinking of nothing special, just enjoying the hot sun on your back with the bounding ocean curlers. Let's say you're with your girlfriend or boyfriend *(it doesn't matter)*, but then it pops into your mind that you'd like to know whether or not you're here, **stop!** Turn around and look where you've been walking. See if there are any footprints right behind you stretching off into the distance, and notice if they return to your feet. If so, it's excellent proof, so breathe a sigh, **you're here**!

If your boyfriend's or girlfriend's footprints are also returning from the far-off distance and leading right to his or her feet, you can reassure him or her, he or she is also here. If both footprints seem to be parallel one another from way back there to your present location, you can also surmise he or she is not only here, but also he or she is **with you.**

If, again, at the beach in your bathing attire, walking away from the hot, setting sun that's giving you a late burn on the back, you notice funny, dark, shadow-like things apparently walking before you that are ultimately connected to your feet, **stop abruptly,** bend the right knee to lift the right foot high in the air. You should notice the shadow-like dark spot on the sand rises too, and only connects to the left foot. Now put the right foot down and raise the left leg and left foot. The shadow does the same. Now, with both feet down, stick out your arms and wave them violently and waggle your head back and forth and then jump up and down. If the shadow does the same, you know the shadow belongs to you and **you are here!**

If you can get your boyfriend or girlfriend to do the same, you can prove to him or her beyond all shadow of a doubt that **he or she is here, too!**

Word of caution! Should you not find a wet nose after sneezing, or you do not see your footprints *(God forbid!!)*, or fail to see your shadow on the beach, be prepared! Strange things can only be imagined! In sneezing, you may have blown yourself into another world. If you don't see footprints, you're obviously not here! That being true, I can only say, *"Godspeed!"* or some other arbitrary phrase. Not seeing your shadow could mean you're an Angel, an agent of God, or a messenger of the Devil, scouring the earth for unseemly ends, or you could be the figment of somebody else's imagination, or, I can't go on! It's too much! You think of things.

However, if you do experience wonderful things like a wet nose, or footprints, or jumping shadows, be like me! Perform the necessary steps to prove to yourself *(and others),* once and for all, **You are truly here!**

Remembrances of my Father

When a cat died he'd put it in a hole in the ground and plant a tree over it. Then, he'd say, *"The cat will make good fertilizer."*

My dad loved plants and worked in his garden. When a plant was doing well, he'd be proud and exclaim his joy. When a plant refused to grow, he'd yank it out and throw it away. He only had time for plants that showed promise.

My dad said, *"See what I'm doing?"*

"Yes," I'd say. "Polishing your shoes."

"Do you see where I'm polishing?"

"Yes. The back."

The lesson was that the whole shoe needed to be polished, not just the part everyone sees.

My dad said, *"When you're working for somebody else, give 'em an extra half hour. You'll always have a job."*

Movement of Continents

I'd like to think about something more exciting, like the drifting of continents. How's that for a starter? Well, continents don't exactly drift; they are more or less continually pushed out of position by molten lava oozing up between long, mid-oceanic cracks. Lava spews out down a long line, solidifies, and then does it again, forcing the Earth's crust ever outward. It's been doing that for 4.6 billion years. Well, all that lava leakage ought to move *something!* It crowds continents against one another such that mountains are formed, and the heat generated is so strong, volcanoes either blow up, scattering molten rock and magma into the air and all over earth's surface, or they erupt more slowly, spewing brilliant, boiling, hot goop that flows down the slopes to harden in the water while cooling to an average temperature. Doesn't that frost your balls?

But then my mind must be holding more than continental movement, but the idea of *continents being pushed continually, and what would seem arbitrarily out of place over Earth's lifetime* is a heady thought, indeed. Where do we go from here? Well! All present living things die, of course, geologically speaking, in a very short time, but the earth will continue rotating, be pulled this way and that by the moon, be heated by a slowly warming sun *(as the sun dies)*, pursue its cosmic fate until in its final stages earth is destroyed by the heat of an expanded, enveloping sun.

What will future Earth be like? I suspect oceans and land will be here for quite a while and life will repeat itself as it's done in the past. Miracles, as now, will continue into the future. Archetypal living forms, like sharks and turtles, may continue to live longer than those less adaptive to a longer life, but as the world turns, life will generate to huge or microscopic forms with everything in between. Life will be of all shapes and colors, and an understanding creature will be blown away by inconceivable complexities, if there is such a future understanding creature.

The Director

"**OK!** Everyone, gather around. Come on now! That's right, in a big circle. In the last scene, you've just given thunderous applause to GINO, the award winner for Outstanding Community Service who just stepped off the stage after his "thank you" speech."

In the next scene, we see just the top of GINO'S bald head over the noisy crowd congratulating him.

"For what the studio's paying you a week, you partygoers are going to have to EARN your $500 a day. I want laughter, ballroom chatter, congratulations to GINO and for God's sake, pretend you're having fun!"

To review the next scene, OTTO, feigning normalcy, quietly descends the stairs. He thinks the award winner, GINO, has killed his brother. He intends to get revenge by killing him in public with a short switchblade jab to the stomach. He wants to stay oblivious and doesn't want the crowd to know what he's up to, so he moves unobtrusively down the stairs to perform his dastardly deed.

"Places, everyone! Lights! Camera! *ACTION!*"

(With laughter and congratulatory noises, the crowd moves around GINO while the camera catches OTTO taking the first few steps down the stairs.)

"CUT! CUT!"

(Crowd stops milling. The actor playing OTTO remains quizzically on the third step down with one foot in the air.)

Don't come down the stairs with your hands in your pockets! Take your hands out of your pockets. OTTO wouldn't do that! Try it again!

(Otto jumps back up to the top of the stairs, ready to go!)

"Crowd ready? *ACTION*!"

(Otto begins again to descend the stairs. One step, two steps, three steps, four steps, foot in the air –)

"CUT! CUT! CUT!"

"OK! Your hands look better, but don't chew gum! The killer doesn't want people to see him. Chewing gum attracts attention! OTTO would not be chewing gum! NO GUM! Throw the gum down here! GLADYS, pick it up. That's right! Use a hanky! Throw it to the stagehand. OK! Ready, everybody?"

"*ACTION!*"

(OTTO makes his first move by stumbling on the first step.)

"CUT! CUT! CUT! CUT!"

That's OK! Try it again!

"*ACTION!*"

(Otto makes is first step, but his white shoelace is flopping over his black shoe.)

"WAIT! WAIT! WAIT!"

"EVERYBODY STOP – CUT! CUT! CUT!"

"For God's sake, let's go over this again. Now, OTTO, you have to understand something! You think GINO'S killed your brother. You loved your brother very much and are going to get revenge on Gino by sticking a knife in his gut, then disappear through the back door. Got that?"

"Crowd! Ready? *ACTION!*"

(Crowd starts noisily moving around GINO as OTTO straightens himself up and stiffly begins to march down three or four steps until --)

"CUT! CUT! CUT! CUT!"

"MY GOD! DON'T WALK LIKE THAT! You look like a robot. Move naturally! Swing your arms a little! Don't hold them straight down at your sides, and don't kick your knee straight out like that! You look like a monster! The aliens have NOT landed! Go on back up and try it again!"

(OTTO tramps back up the stairs, turns around and swings his arms to loosen them up and taking a deep breath and letting it out slowly, pulls up his pants, hunkers down, narrows his eyes, and glancing to the left and right, begins to tiptoe down the stars.)

"CUT! CUT! CUT!"

"OTTO! OTTO! OTTO! Do we have to go over this again? Don't squint your eyes! You're not Peter Lorre! Cut the Stanislavski kick! Can't you get it? You don't want to be noticed by the public and you are going to get revenge by knifing the guy playing the heavy! Now do it again! My God! It's noon already!"

(OTTO bounds up the stairs two at a time, turns around and readies himself for the next take. He's distraught. His tie is not straight. His hair is loose over one eye and his shoestring is beginning to loosen.)

"Lights! Camera! *ACTION!*"

(OTTO moves down the stairs, step by step, brushing his hair out of his eyes, but not too much. So far he's doing well, and gets five or six steps down, and the director whispers to the cameraman.)

"Move in to get a close-up shot of OTTO'S hand and knife moving out of his pocket. He's doing it! He's doing it! That's it! That's it!"

(Caught by the camera in a close-up view, from his right-hand pocket, OTTO pulls a glistening switchblade knife, evidence of the audacity of his soon to be performed crime. It's going perfectly until OTTO'S fingers catch his pocket lining and he fumbles the knife. It falls clattering down the stairs, and bounces over the side where, after a long pause, it hits the floor with an unflattering BANG and skitters, spinning, under the stairs. At the same time, OTTO grabs the railing with both hands and barely keeps himself from falling.)

"CUT! CUT! CUT! CUT!"

"MY GOD! CAN'T YOU TAKE A SIMPLE KNIFE OUT OF YOUR SIMPLE POCKET WITHOUT DROPPING IT? Don't say you're sorry! My God! Get back up there! Are you trying to sabotage this take! Are you a spy from another network? This is taking all day! I'm exhausted! One more time! But, we're not quitting until we get this right!"

(GLADYS returns the gun to OTTO, straightens his tie, relaces his shoe and pats dust off his suit. OTTO once again makes it to the top of the stairs. GINO and the crowd are bored and sweating under their costumes and heavy makeup, solaced only by remembering pay for overtime. OTTO stands at the top with one finger picking his nose.)

"LIGHTS! CAMERA! *ACTION!*"

(OTTO trips on the first step, grabs for a railing, swings his head sharply to the side, loses his balance and falls backward, clattering head over knees and elbows – BANG! POW! DING! PATOOEY! – To the bottom of the steps where he bumps his head on the floor and lies there, face up, visibly dazed.

Actors rush to give him help! GLADYS dashes from the wings shouting, "GIVE 'EM AIR! GIVE 'EM AIR!" The director drops his megaphone, turns his head, and walks disgustedly away.

Presently, order is established. OTTO has one arm over GLADYS' shoulder and the other around his head. They dizzily wobble here and there at the bottom of the stairs.)

GLADYS lets OTTO go off stage for a rest.

(OTTO limps off stage.)

"GLADYS! GLADYS! GLADYS! You are a fine prop lady, but I know you can also act. I'm sure you'll be as good as anyone in this part. Mount the stairs and show us how it's done!"

(GLADYS goes to the top of the stairs and stands poised, ready for the take.)

"LIGHTS! CAMERA! ACTION!"

(Knife in a skirt pocket, GLADYS descends the stairs calmly and deliberately, calling no attention to herself. She is completely unnoticeable to everyone in the congratulatory crowd. Halfway down the stairs, she reveals to the audience, in a white-gloved hand, the gleam of her treacherous weapon before silently replacing it. At the bottom of the stairs, she easily merges with the crowd while making her twisting way to GINO, where she plunges the (retractable) knife deep into his surprised gut and *disappears into the crowd. As GINO slips to the floor, she moves easily towards the back exit and disappears into the night.)*

"CUT!"

"THAT'S A WRAP! Thanks, everyone! You can go home now!"

"Joe! We've got to change the part of the brother to the part of the sister! We'll call her OLGA!"

"GLADYS! GLADYS! YOU'VE GOT THE PART!"

"WRITER! WRITER!"

Now, where's the cookies at?

So What!

In response to looking at the sun, I had the urge to sneeze. I inhaled every ounce of air my organism could take, closed my eyes and expelled tiny droplets with such force it could raise the god of sleep. Accompanied by a piercing light, a pain in my head and swirling clouds, I was quickly relieved by vanishing clouds and evaporating mists and found myself sitting on a chair at the top of a pole thrusting 50' in the air from a beach of sand on the edge of limitless water. The day was overcast. It had been raining and off in the distance large creatures were lumbering about.

Fifty were in dark shades of blue, brown, black and green; though stumbling about, they looked like smooth-skinned sloths and were the size of elephants. From a jumbled mess, they formed themselves into rows of ten, like a military marching band, and followed each other with musical barking foreign to my ears. I suspect I even heard harmony! Perhaps even four-part harmony. They hypnotized me and seemed to focus my attention on large, colored, marching beasts and musical barking in four-part harmony.

Presently the clouds darkened and I was struck with a tremendous downpour. An umbrella magically appeared to cover my head and when the rain stopped, the sloth-like creatures broke formation, paired in two lines and marched into the forest and out of sight. Clouds broke with patches of sunlight while I sat under my umbrella. The sun moved swiftly to the west drying the sand. The sand turned to dust. The dust triggered a sneeze and I blew myself back into the real world!

In Between

Since I know many 50's songs and love to sing in the shower or car, and have a somewhat out-of-tune voice with limited range, I jokingly tell my kids they can either have a CD recording of *Doug Rucker Sings* or a CD of *Beethoven's 5th*, recorded at 45 rpm. This breaks me up, but they never laugh. I'm not clear about how they take it.

I guess what I offered is something like putting them in a position of being "*between the Devil and the deep blue sea.*" At my age I feel it's time I get my say, and in my definition the Devil is a fallen angel; a supernatural being located downward in another location and the host of a fiery place I'd do just as well without. The sea calls forth vast quantities of water I sometimes can *"see into,"* the color of the sky with connotations of relentlessly blown waves, which, though delightful upon occasion, can at times be stubbornly careless and unforgiving – such as if I were to drown.

Both scenarios are like being caught "*between a rock and a hard place.*" Either alternative is disastrous.

You:
"What does this have to do with anything?"
Me:
"I'm trying to discuss that difficult area between two or more points."
You:
"*Why?*"
Me:
"Because there is more to be said."
You:
"*What?*"
Me:
"Because, while most decisions are easy, the hardest are

difficult. Consider an easy one; I'm going to cross the street, but a car is coming, so I *decide* to wait until the car passes, then I'll cross the street."

Consider a harder one: There's heavy traffic at a busy intersection. I'm in a *hurry*, but the light is against me. I decide to either: (1) Wait for a lull, then jaywalk; or (2) Wait for the light *(which means I might be late)*, then cross.

Being in a *hurry and why I'm in a hurry, heavy traffic,* and *going against the light* are added complexities that further complicate the choice. Consequences must always be paid, and getting there on time and the possibility of being hit by a car are inextricably related and must be considered.

No matter what choice I make, personalities come into play. Am I a *risk taker,* or do I *play it safe*? Am I *thoughtless,* or *mindful,* or an *average combination*? What would a *thoughtful, mindful* person do?

I'm a percentage kind of a guy and I believe things are never either all one way or all the other. I'm sure I could play it like this: I'm in a hurry, but it's not life or death. There's heavy traffic, but I'm sure I can dart between the cars. I'm mindful and won't move until I'm sure. Go!

And now I'm compelled to write something on integrity. Cars, trees, pavement, animals, birds, fish, mountains, ocean, air, clouds, stones and giraffes all have integrity. Only people with a cerebral cortex are limited in the integrity department. Only with the reasoning ability of the recently developed cerebral cortex can we figure out how to deceive for profit.

But now that I think of it, the thought reminds me of a funny (?) little two-paragraph story I wrote called *Benny the Bunny and Ripper the Shepherd*. Benny, a vegetarian bunny, grew fat and happy eating grandma's carrots. Ripper saw him one day, pounced on him and ate him on the spot. Later, Ripper went home, was fed and fell asleep by the fire. That was the end of the Benny the Bunny story, also being the archetypal story of all living planetary creatures they both had integrity.

By my limited understanding, essentially, there are three parts of the brain: the *automatic/parasympathetic nervous systems (handling things we don't have to think about – breathing, digestion, elimination, fight or flight, etc.)*, the *unconscious mind (that part of the mind of which we are not conscious – repressed feelings, dreams, forgotten memories, etc.)* and the *cerebral cortex (*a *thin, outer layer of gray matter that handles the higher functions of the brain – sensation, voluntary muscle movement, thought, reasoning, memory, etc.)*.

The human brain developed over millions of years of selective habitation. Basically, the unconscious brain is the collective unconscious.

You finish the rest!

Soul

The soul is the essence and meaning of everything in it.

The Universe has a soul.

A soul is a feeling and not matter.

Non-living things have a soul usually felt for them by other living beings.

A car, airplane, telescope and radio can have a soul if felt as having one by a person living.

Since everyone is different and has a different feeling, no two feelings are the same.

I know nothing that is not in my consciousness.

For a soul to exist for its own or others, a living being must experience it.

This talk is about humans having feelings of souls and not about not human beings having souls.

Souls are only attached to matter.

If the universe has a soul, everything in the Universe has a soul including all of matter.

This includes atoms, electrons, protons, Higgs bosons, neutrinos and all the matter so labeled including individual photons, etc., in normal and quantum physics.

Soul 115

To me, not only humans and living entities have souls, but also non-living entities. I feel everything, living or not living, has a soul.

I feel there are souls in dogs, cats, plants, rocks, oceans, clouds, mountains, etc.

If things come into existence and wink out apparently into nothingness, that piece of matter had a soul while it was here. If no one knew about it, it had no soul.

If matter winked out, the matter's soul also winked out. *(Though memory of the soul might be there, what isn't there still isn't there.)*

If every individual thing in the Universe has a soul *(a feeling by some living thing with knowledge of each piece of matter)*, it includes humans, animals, reptiles, birds, aquatic life, plants in air and water, rocks, gravel, sand, basalt, etc. Since portions of the Universe consist of matter, a single stone in gravel, a particle of sand, a virus and an amoeba have souls.

The Universe contains 23% dark matter causing the Universe to contract, and 72% dark energy causing the Universe to expand. Being within the boundaries of the Universe dark matter and dark energy have souls.

Do souls ever change over the lifetime of matter? Yes and no! Souls are born along with matter and remain the soul of the matter. If the matter is a rock, my feeling of soul remains for that particular rock. If the rock is crushed, making new particles and souls, my remembrance of soul may be retained, but, since a rock has no ability to detect a feeling, the rock doesn't know it lost its soul. Only a former observer with a memory would sense the feeling of the soul and remember it, love it or be indifferent to it or hate it.

When I die, my soul dies with me. Except that those who formerly knew me might retain or remember my essence or what I stood for, which they would call my soul. If another never knew my existence, my soul would not be missed and for him my soul never existed. *(You can't miss what you don't know.)*

Does a rock, or a mountain, or a glacier, desert, ocean, pond or river have a soul? Yes! Though it may be made up of lots of different things like those complications inside a human, animal, plant, bird or fish, the complete object and what each thing is made of is part of its soul.

Can the feeling of soul change over time? Yes. Sculpting the heads of four American presidents into the top of a mountain changed the original mountain's soul to one including sculptures of four presidential heads.

An alcoholic drink is created through the mixture of vermouth, vodka and olive juice, giving a martini a single soul made out of three components, all of which, before having been made into a martini, used to have a soul.

Other examples are damming a river, making a computer, creating an island or making pancakes, etc.

Are there degrees of soul? Is there a 100% soul, or a 50% soul, or a 2% soul? It depends on the feelings of who feels the questionable soul. Some may think of the soul of a fly at 2% is less important than the soul of an elephant, at 75% or one of Einstein at 99% as against a housekeeper, at 75%.

Are some souls expendable and others not? The same as whether or not the feelings of the single person are expendable.

Are their important souls and unimportant souls? It depends on who has the feeling.

Should souls be evaluated and their fate determined by other souls? Yes and no. Fate decrees we feel souls or not, and deal with souls however we like, whether we like it or not.

Common Sense Religion

My contractor friend and his wife were raised by Mormons and continued in the Mormon faith and have raised their children as Mormons. I have a beloved client who had Catholic parents. She continued in the Catholic faith and raised her seven kids Catholic. One of my oldest friends had parents who were devoted to the Christian Science religion and my friend became a Christian Scientist and raised his children in the same faith. By my experience, I understand the religion of the parents is usually passed down to the children who then pass it down to their own children, and this is how traditions and lasting religions are made.

Brand new in the world, small children are unable to fend for their personal safety and are dependent for survival on their parents. Without the love and caring parents devote to their children, they'd die. If they want to be raised in peace and harmony, children, with no choice in their immediate family, are either forced, required, or want to comply with the wishes of the elders. What the parents know and believe is the only critical influence in what the child knows and believes. Before the age of ten, a child must respond and conform to messages it hears from the parents. If he or she doesn't, the penalty is huge; his or her personal self is diminished, or in the worst case, destroyed.

Therefore, it's reasonable to expect that grown-up children, that is, those who are old enough to marry, having successfully navigated their own days of dependency, will know and believe something very similar to those beliefs taught them by their parents, and since their parents' belief was already predetermined by their parents' ways of knowing and living life, will raise their own children in the only way they learned how: with the same beliefs as their parents. Never was it so true that

Common Sense Religion

what goes around comes around. A continuous way of judging the world becomes traditional, and in most cases whatever religion a child learns, eventualy he teaches.

Looking at my own life, I've noticed I have no church-going religion. It's only after being exposed to people who regularly go to church that I've come to ask myself why *I* don't go to church or have a religion. Though I don't belong to a church, I do have powerful thoughts and passionate philosophies and suspect I don't look or feel much different from anyone else. I've functioned in a lasting business of my own for well over 50 years and I'm certainly religious when it comes to caring about my self and caring about my family and work. Do I, or do I not have a religion? I decided to ask myself how *I* was raised. The answer to that question might let me know what I believe and how I differ, if I do, from my religious and church-going friends. It seemed an act of common sense to look into my own childhood and see how *I* was raised and how *I* came to *my* beliefs and following what seems to be the normal rule, how I would raise *my own* children. If I do that, I'm asking myself about my parents' religion and my grandparents' religion, or lack of religion, to discover the aptitude of my own beliefs and my own religion.

Let me say at the beginning, I have some strong beliefs about humanity and the world. To illustrate what I think, I'd like to use the words of Henry James, written in letters to his sons ...

"Every man who has reached his intellectual teens begins to suspect that life is no farce; that it is not a genteel comedy ever; that it flowers and fructifies out of the profoundest tragic depths of the essential dearth in which its roots are plunged. The natural inheritance of everyone who is capable of spiritual life is an unsubdued forest where the wolf howls and the obscene bird of night chatters."

Beginnings

At six years old, in the furnace room of our four-story brick apartment building while I was trying to get a small box open, my father, then the janitor for our 4-story brick apartment, said to my mother, *"Mother, let Doug alone, he can figure it out for himself."* This phrase planted the seed in my brain that *I could possibly figure things out for myself.* Later, trying to manipulate a hammer and nail, father said, "*Use your ingenuity.*" Again, my dad planted the seed to help me figure things out, possibly that I had something called *ingenuity.* While that was running through my mind, I remember another time when pointing to his head, he said, "*Use your common sense."* Evidently, I also had something within me, called *common sense.*

I began to suspect *I could figure things out for myself using ingenuity and common sense.*

I now suspect my religion might be called . . .

The Religion of Common Sense

The eldest of seven, my father was forced to quit school in the middle of seventh grade and go to work to help raise a family of nine. His family attended no religious services, but dad always used the word *"Lord"* with reverence and respect. He looked kindly on all people whether they went to church or not.

My mother's mother was a devout Catholic who attended services regularly. My mother's father was a professional journalist and editor who believed along with his colleagues, Mark Twain, Jack London, Marcel Proust, Bertrand Russell, and H. L. Menchen, in atheism. My mother, as the eldest child with a strong literary bent, was *"Daddy's little girl."* My mother, while being loving and gentle towards others, leaned heavily toward her journalist dad's belief in atheism.

Dave, my four-years-younger brother and I were neither prevented from nor encouraged to go to church, nor was there any opportunity to attend church services since nobody went. We were raised by a father who had no formal religious training and a gentle, loving mother influenced by her mother and the Catholic religion. At heart, as *"Daddy's little girl,"* she was an atheist. My mother being open-minded had an acceptance of all people and a regard for all religions.

Common Sense Religion – Three Parts

The habit of attending religious ceremonies and obtaining a religious education are usually one of the earliest of childhood experiences. From my early life I seem to have just three pieces of knowledge that affected my grownup life: *(1) Figure things out for myself; (2) using ingenuity; (3) with common sense.* These worked together to form my lifetime religion.

Figuring things out for myself by using ingenuity and common sense required special talents. Whether I had those, or not, I did not know. Using common sense was something I thought I understood.

Of course, using *"common sense"* involved other qualities like reasonableness, understanding, education and empathy. Evidently, I had to have some of those, too.

If touching a hot frying pan with my finger would burn me, then I shouldn't do that. When jumping off a cliff, I might break a leg or die, so I shouldn't do that. While driving, crossing the double line might get everyone killed, so I should not do that.

I know what I'm not! I'm not a Christian Scientist, Mormon, Catholic, Protestant, Muslim, Jew, Indian, Buddhist, Seventh-Day Adventist, or a Jehovah's Witness. Perhaps I may have made up my own religion that some might think too simple. It's called the *Common Sense Religion,* which, to me, means *"figuring things out using ingenuity and common sense."*

Commandments

Even without having religious training, I did live my life adhering to almost all of the Ten Commandments.

The Ten Commandments are: *having no other God before the theoretical "only one," making no carved images of what I think God might look like, not taking God's name in vain, remembering to relax and pray on Sunday, honoring mom and dad, committing no murder, adultery or robbery, bearing no false witness and not coveting another's wife.*

I said *"almost"* all the Ten Commandments because, while still immature at 26 years old, I married the mother of my children. Twenty-five years later, my family was severely unhappy, and I divorced and remarried someone who'd made the same mistake. My new wife corrected her lifetime error and I corrected mine.

What follows is my analysis of the Ten Commandments.

1 Thou shalt have no other Gods before me. If God is the Universal Force, I have no other God.

2 Thou shalt make no carved images. It's hard to make a carving of the Universal Force. It's already pretty well been carved.

3 Thou shalt not take the Lord's name in vain. Because the Universal force is incapable of caring, it makes little difference whether to swear its name or not. If it could be heard, it wouldn't change.

4 Thou shalt remember the Sabbath day. Any day could be the big-bang day, or the Universal Force's Sabbath day. I wasn't there and only know what I think is the best of what's known.

5 Thou shalt honor thy father and mother. Fortunately, I had by all good standards, outstanding parents, and shall always honor them.

6 Thou shalt commit no murder. This is ridiculous! I don't need to pray not to kill somebody. It's the last thing on my mind, but it depends on circumstances. If someone injures my kid, I'll not be responsible for what I'll do. This is a Human thing. Sometimes murder is a human species thing, such as if my

family is threatened, I will defend them and do what needs to be done.

7 Thou shalt not commit adultery. I've got to bend on that one. My new wife and I left troubled 25-year marriages, having made lifetime commitments far before we were emotionally ready. In our new marriage, we've had over 35 years of wedded bliss, with seven children and eight grandchildren, all unified and happy. Sometimes it's necessary to correct a bad mistake.

8 Thou shalt not steal. What's there to steal? If you're ready to die from lack of food and water, I'd say OK, steal. I'm a fortunate man. I've got a good wife and good kids and am financially endowed with enough money to make it through.

9 Thou shalt not bear false witness. I've had false witness borne against me. It's not pretty. I'd never do that to someone else. How does that fit with *"Do unto others as you would have them do unto you?"* Bearing false witness blackens both names.

10 Thou shalt not covet thy neighbor's wife. I have to give that one a mea culpa because I did and my new wife coveted another's husband. Eventually everyone was happier including children of the unmarried spouses. Where is it written, *"Thou shalt not learn from one's mistakes?"*

Now I'd like to interpret a prayer my mother taught me when I was a child.

"Now I lay me down to sleep,
I pray the Lord my soul to keep.
If I should die before I wake,
I pray the Lord my soul to take."

Interpretation:

Line 1 – I'm being put to bed.

Line 2 – Even though I've just begun my life, I'm praying or asking or hoping that some powerful personage that I don't know will keep my soul for me, if I have a soul, because, evidently I couldn't keep it myself and mom and dad can't keep another's soul.

Line 3 – I speculate about dying before morning even though mom and dad thought I'd probably make it through the night. Death at six years old was far beyond my imagination.

Line 4 – I was encouraged to verbalize that it was my prayer, hope, desire, that IF, as a youngster, I were to pass on to a better world, the powerful personage whom I don't know would accept my soul, which I was not sure what one was or if I had one, and keep it, presumably, in a better place.

Prayer allows the one who prays to clarify his subject. It is similar to hope, but more important because it's also a verbalized medium of expression of desire. It can be intimate, or altruistic, or selfish, or desperate, but in every case it clarifies the thoughts, feelings and position of the one who prays and more firmly establishes that persons wants and desires that more easily provoke an action to achieve the desired end.

It is certain that it is beneficial in the majority of cases, that if the ill, injured, or unhappy person knows he or she is being prayed for, he or she knows those praying persons care for them and knowing they are cared for to whatever degree encourages self worth that enhances the person's natural self-healing ability. I can't imagine prayer that is hoping, wishing, praying or desiring of a positive outcome is not extremely beneficial to the one praying.

Another thought: It's possible for someone to pray a rival baseball team would lose, or doctors practicing abortion would be jailed, or we pray to keep the death penalty. People are good and bad, but all are free to pray.

More Commandments?

I think there should be more than Ten Commandments because they make common sense and would be vital to the whole planet.

A simple analysis: The earth is the mother of all living things that exist on it, including the Ebola and AIDS viruses, piranhas, Covid-19, 135 million years of dinosaurs, slime, rot, feces and malted milk and pie. If earth is the mother, then every living thing has the earth as its mother, and every living thing as a sibling, so killing something is like killing a brother or sister or father or uncle. Of course, if we are permitted to be born and live on earth, it is under the condition that we kill something to eat. Don't kill the messenger. I'd like to be wrong. We must accept the good with the bad.

There are Ten Commandments, shouldn't there be more?

(11) Learn from your mistakes.

(12) "Do unto all living things, humans, plants, animals, reptiles, fish, serpents, insects, germs, birds, etc., including water, earth, and atmosphere, etc., as you would have them do unto you."

Of course, mankind is part carnivore and seen by the make of his alimentary tract is an omnivore and is unalterably constructed to eat meat as well as vegetables and can't get out of it. Carnivores and omnivores have to eat other living beings. It's a fact.

Man as a Species

Common sense tells me that man, like lions and tigers and bears, is a *species*. Almost all species have two eyes, two legs, two arms, one head, two eyes, two ears, one nose, and one method of procreation. Endowed with a miracle almost no other animal has, humans have the remarkable ability to remember the past and speculate on the future. Humans don't possess any special capabilities like going to heaven when we die. *"In a single tick of the cosmic clock, I'm strata."* In figuring things out using my ingenuity and common sense, there is no evidence for heaven. Belief or preference is too small and not a substantial answer. In the Common Sense Religion, when a member of a species dies, he or she is gone! The party's over! I've seen road kill and human fossils locked in rock and ancient strata.

Nature, however, has specifically designed us to eat meat. It defies the Religion of Common Sense to battle such a specific reality. If another animal needed me to die for its sustenance, I'd want him to be swift and gentle, then thoroughly clean up. Shouldn't we be so empathetic regarding animals we need to eat?

What about curiosity? Shouldn't there be a Commandment such as:

(13) *"Thou shalt investigate and explore everything of which you are capable."*
Mankind does that anyway. In fact mankind is paranoid about it. What with a 26-mile cyclotron to explode *"no-seeums,"* a permanent space station and the Hubble telescope to examine the universe, the Internet, air travel, railroads, cars, skyscrapers, MRI machines, cruise ships and nuclear energy, we're certainly making stupendous strides in exploring and investigating everything of which we are capable. I can't imagine a commandment like, *"Thou shalt not use all your explorative abilities."* Like procreation, us humans are going to do it anyway.

(14) *"Thou shalt look inward to examine yourself to see if your motives make the world a happier or less happy place."*
That's a heavy one. It means I have to look at what, where and why I do what I do before I do it. It's *"common sense"* and the rule is *think before I do*. To think before you do, it is important so you:

Understand the Whole

In writing **Common Sense Religion**, it is necessary for me to understand the *whole* because *"What I think"* involves the *whole* and how can the whole *not* influence what I think? Not understanding the whole is a recipe for disaster.

It's not my intention to include petty thoughts that bore you *(or me)*, but I've tried to pick the essentials of *"what I think"* so a more complete understanding will occur to each of us.

I came to thinking in terms of the *"whole"* through my 54-year career as an architect doing new homes and remodeling in Malibu. To be a good architect, I need to *"get the whole picture."* The owner doesn't have the whole picture, he just wants a house. The contractor says, *"Show me what to build, and I'll build it."* The bureaucratic agencies have rules to be followed, and they say, *"Show me what you propose, and if it complies, we'll stamp it."* In the process, these three essential figures don't get the whole picture. If they don't get it, who gets it? It has to be the architect. That's why I get the big bucks.

I have to know all the ins and outs of each of the three divisions, and keep everyone smiling to produce a life work of which I'm proud. Since people build buildings, if I'm the decisive person, the building is a reflection of me and who I am. Who I am looks back at me as a finished building. To produce something of which I'm proud involves imagination, sensitivity to the owner and the environment, the cost of the project, and whether the owners and I can agree for a couple of years to get the project done.

Because there are many solutions to a problem, I like to think in scenarios. I often say, *"Let's list all the different ways we can meet the purpose, put them on the table, then choose one."* This usually works because everyone gets a say and a joint solution is usually agreeable.

Therefore, I have included seeing the whole in my views of my life. Of course no one can ever get the whole picture. It's too big, too miraculous, too astounding, but it's my intention to understand it to the degree of my capability. Perhaps another commandment I might add is;

(15) "I shalt understand the whole of the universe to the top of my capability."

Greatest Adventures

Socrates is supposed to have said that all he really was, was the extent of his own ignorance. Christopher Hitchens comments about this in his own book and tells us, *"This to me is still the definition of an educated person."* It means, then, if we subtract a person's ignorance, what's leftover is either nothing or his education.

In the **Religion of Common Sense**, I have chosen my own piece of philosophy: *"The greatest adventures lie within the realm of my own ignorance."* New knowledge, then, is the great adventure, optimistic in resolve, educational in spirit.

Keeping an open mind allows both pleasant and unpleasant facts to enter, and that means my experience of life is broadened. A broadened experience of life means I know more, have felt more feelings, and have learned more thought-provoking ideas leading me to greater creativity, greater depth, and a life that is richer, more fulfilling and complete. Therefore, a 16th commandment might be:

(16) Keep an open mind.

Definitions of Knowing and Believing:

I *know* an open mind is better than a closed mind. How do I know? I'm in great sympathy with deceased Dr. David Viscott's definition of *knowing*. *"Knowing is the truth from a certain perspective."* So, I *do* know things. But what I *know* is what I *believe*. My definition of belief is also Dr. Viscott's definition. Belief is *"knowing something is so, whether or not it is."*

To me, knowing is strongly related to *faith, confidence* and *truth*. I know the sun will come up because it comes up every day for my lifetime. Therefore, I have *faith* it will come up. I have *confidence* it will come up. And this *faith* and *confidence* adds up to my *truth*, and the truth is *"the sun will come up."* To me, faith must be based on a percentage of past performance. Faith based on *no* past performance is blind faith.

A Percentage Kind of a Guy

Faith, being a condition where I can have a lot of faith, or have a moderate amount of faith, or hardly any faith, is a matter of percentages. If I eat, my hunger is assuaged. If I drink, my thirst is assuaged. If I work hard at something, I love that people will pay me and, hence, give me a place to live, have a family, and complete my life. I have faith it will rain during the rainy season, or snow during winter, or be hot in the sand in summer. Of course, the sun coming up every day is one thing of which I'm completely certain. Faith, for me, depends on percentages. I had faith it would rain during the rainy season for the next two years. It did not. Sometimes I can be disappointed in my faith. Unless it's like the sun coming up, faith is chancy, and for me it depends on what it did in the past.

Following Parents Beliefs

Each person, male or female, is born at a different time when the earth has spun on its axis an additional nine months, and time, moving in a straight line as it does, is nine months or so in advance from where it was before. Each new baby born at each new time has its own qualities of mind, body, spirit and soul, including an arbitrary combination of their parents' mind and body.

Beginning of the World

In the very beginning, the unimaginable happened! A tiny *nothing* exploded into an unimaginably large number of particles and energy and other stuff that eventually became light, electromagnetic forces, solid matter, gravity, dark matter, dark energy, micro-matter, and other things only to be read about in science magazines. Unbelievably, after the big bang, it took millions of years before there was light! Over billions of years, that energy made an unimaginable number of galaxies, black holes, giant dwarfs, quasars, nebulae and clouds of stellar dust, one of which is our average-sized Milky Way, still expanding and moving out into space and containing our solar system. It has the sun and eight or nine rotating planets, including Earth, with various moons.

Eight-ninths of the age of our planet *(four billion years)* went by before grass began to grow, and when that happened, oxygen, the major element needed to produce life as we know it, was released into the atmosphere. Slowly, fish, lizards, birds, reptiles and tiny mammals inhabited the earth, culminating in dinosaurs, masters of the planet for over 135 million years. Then, a six-mile diameter comet smashed into the Yucatan peninsula, creating a black cloud that enveloped the earth, darkening the sky and freezing the dinosaurs and most everything on it.

Millions of years passed before warm-blooded animals developed to take the place of dinosaurs, and about 100,000 years ago, a primitive creature arrived, resembling mankind. For 90,000 years, mankind lived in tribes, killing other living creatures for food, including deer, pigs, fowl, fish, elephants, etc. After the ice age, 11,000 years ago, and after the saber-tooth tigers, mastodons and mammoths had been hunted to extinction, mankind discovered he could keep domestic animals, goats, sheep, cows, chickens, etc., and plant corn, wheat, beans, tomatoes and vegetables for food. Catching and eating wild creatures became less important because man was able to survive the winter and lean years due to the food he stored.

Earth is one of the byproducts of the big bang. Considering everything, Earth is *our* Mother. I live on Mother Earth! In the **Religion of Common Sense,** with Earth as the mother and the big bang as the father, everything living or non-living on the Earth is my sister or brother. I'd like to take it a step farther and say, *"And they should be treated that way!"*

Process and Context

I believe what is to be accomplished today should be in the context of what's happening today. Certainly, what happened yesterday is already recorded for history and yesterday. The alternative *(recreating the past)* is a waste of precious time. To build an aircraft using yesterday's methods is ridiculous and doesn't meet the criteria of gained knowledge and Common Sense. Why not use the new, the tested, and the best that's available? Intelligence and common sense gives us the opportunity to use only the latest proven methods to produce a transportation system that flies through the air with the greatest of ease, allowing minimum fuel and advanced speed. Certainly, I wouldn't want to buy a 10-year-old car or fly in a 30-year-old plane or travel in a train of the *"1920s."* Not to be up-to-date is a negative mark against the progress and miracle of mankind.

Time and Reality

Any time I snap my fingers, I capture reality. It's un-exciting, repetitious, and a waste of creativity and intelligence to demand today the reality of a former time. Sometime long ago when someone else snapped his or her fingers. Someone asked who would be the more mature, a 20-year old or an eight-year old, presuming, I expect, that he assumed I would naturally say the elder, but my answer was that they were both mature for their age. When I was a child, I thought like a child; when I was a young adult, I thought as a young adult. As an old man, I think as an old man. Of course, I've known some young people with greater maturity than their older friends, all attesting to the fact that people are different.

(It makes me unhappy to say the computer age has passed me by.)

"Correct Me if I'm Wrong"

In any discussion I may have on religion and my passionate philosophy of life on earth, it's good for me to continue my completed comments with a comment directed to any thinking listener: *"Correct me if I'm wrong."* If the comment remains unanswered, I'll assume tentative agreement and continue with my argument. If a colleague corrects me, I'm personally bound to listen carefully. I might learn something and correct my thinking. The worst that can happen is that whatever I've said will be more fully rounded out and therefore better understood, perhaps by both of us.

My Philosophy

Viewed through the most sophisticated microscope, matter, that final concrete, indivisible substance upon which I'd welcome basing my philosophy, is absent. Each of the atoms of a rock has protons swirling about them. Is then a rock alive? And when you take the most sophisticated microscope and examine the atom, or protons, which won't stand still for experiments, as the ultimate building block for all things, they disappear into infinity of nothingness. Life is, like they say, a kind of music.

Perhaps the big bang theory is plausible since, where there's no substance it occupies no space and can be crowded quite closely. Recent investigations have shown *no-see-ums* in space called *black matter*, essential to keep galaxies from imploding or exploding. If matter attracts matter, the stars, planets and moons of a galaxy account for only a fraction of what is necessary to hold them together. Black matter, of course, holds them together, and evidently does the trick.

My philosophy is that we are in a musical dream made up of our night sky and this planet, and though we continually discover more, we continually know less. If we assume we are in a miraculous dream with galaxies and suns and planets, land and water, humans, plants and animals, we live in a miraculous terrarium, protected from -400 degrees centigrade by a slim and deteriorating layer of gas. What would my philosophy be then? Answer: I accept all the things my five senses tell me as true from my standpoint and that this is in the nature of the human species. I accept that trees grow to fulfillment, mate, reseed and die, as do all plants, humans and animals. I accept that a table, though a musical dream, is in fact a hard substance, because that's the way it looks and feels. Philosophy starts with Life. There is faith, trust, love and the body. Love is the key ingredient to life and is good. Without faith and trust there is no love and therefore there is no good. Lack of love, to a greater or lesser degree, I would call evil. Good, then is defined by evil, for without evil there would be no good and vice versa. Therefore, I have faith and trust that there will be good and evil, and love and no love, to a greater or lesser degree.

Reality

"Make reality your friend." That phrase, coined by Marge, has been recurring to me lately in regard to another one, which is its opposite, *"Live in Fantasy."* According to Marge, if I do not face reality, I'm living in fantasy.

Fantasy seems to be an idea more acceptable to some than others. I'll give you an example:

I know I'll pass that test even though I've not studied. Well, of course, I took the test and flunked. Why? Because I didn't study. I didn't face reality which was the facts. I didn't move the boat because my oars weren't in the water. Why? I was tired of the subject. I didn't need that course to graduate, anyway. I was out last night drinking and too "bombed" to worry about it. I didn't like my parents forcing me to study a hateful course, and this was my passive-aggressive method of revolt. There can be a million reasons why I took the path of flunking, not all of which may be known to my conscious mind.

What if I didn't pass the course because my unconscious mind wouldn't allow it? *(That's a reason the left brain might justify the wishy-washiness of the right brain. Of course, the unconscious mind might be working for the organism's best interests. I'll never know.)*

There are an infinite number of reasons why I may not live in reality. *(I have to ask myself at this time: Whose reality? My mother's? My own? My dad's reality?)*

Nevertheless, digression excused, to live in reality is to, GULP, face the facts!

I try! I try! But there are so many reasons why I can't. There could be old, unconscious issues stored away in my unexamined mind forcing me not to study, or just an ineffective conscious mind, lazy excuses or not being smart. Yes! Ignorance could be my problem. I may be too dumb to face reality!

I might visualize a conversation with myself, *"Heck! I thought I was doing OK and now I'm bummed! They tell me I'm not facing reality."* It seems simplistic to ask why I, or any person, might live inside a fantasy world while reality is so blatantly ever-present, unless, to me, reality isn't so blatantly ever-present.

From a world standpoint, at any given second, reality exists! At this tiny, infinitesimal moment in time, there's a worldwide pandemic. Wounded soldiers are suffering or recuperating, icebergs are slipping into the sea, the world population is growing alarmingly, America moves deeper into debt. More countries are developing a nuclear bomb, 50% of the world's population suffers from malnutrition, and only 1%, so the latest study goes, has a working computer to help them think, etc. This is the present world reality and all the wishing, thinking, hoping and praying cannot make the change. Reality is what it is!

Reality is what it is!!!

About Death

The French female writer, George Sand *(1804-1876),* speaking of her former atheist tutor about to die, heard him ... *"fervently uphold the authority of the church. ... He had been unable to accept the horror of nothingness."* The words, *"horror of nothingness"* symbolizes the value of life and awareness as the ultimate miracle!

I don't *fear* death, because after death I'll no longer have awareness. I will not think, feel, see, hear or taste, or have strange feelings something's curiously odd. When the five gorgeous senses are *"kaput,"* there *is* no awareness.

Before I die, I do fear being uncomfortable. Before my pacemaker, I almost fainted at the computer. My irregular heart decided to pause for four seconds and blood didn't get to my brain. Things went black and I slumped over my keyboard in an almost faint. If the heart can stop for so short a time almost causing death, what fragile creatures we must be. I knew that dying because of a heart stoppage is a piece of cake. I faint, become unconscious, and while I'm unconscious, I sleep and die. No strain, no gain, but no pain! How simple is that?

Of course there's the reverse of the story. Long ago, my former wife had cancer of the lungs and brain. She struggled with physical/mental agonies for a year. In the last stages, increased morphine produced a coma-like existence and eventually became useless in stopping pain. After a long and disheartening effort in the hospital she gave up the ghost and died.

Then there is the story of her father who eventually died of Alzheimer's desease after seven long years in the Veterans Hospital. The bedridden years were difficult for the living and the pleasures of life for the victim were zero. But how am I to judge the value of life to a person so committed? I can only assume.

I don't *fear* death. I fear a *painful* death.

Then there was the story about a person given devastating news.

Doctor. *"You have only 12 weeks to live."*

Patient. *"Will I be in pain?"*

Doctor, *"No. You'll function normally for 11 weeks, but the last week, you'll have enormous pain."*

Patient, *"Can I skip the last week?"*

My mother avowed euthanasia years before she died at almost 94. She'd expressed herself previously in a newspaper article showing there are times when a widow has lived a good life, i.e. childhood, young adulthood, marriage, family, children, retirement, and old age, and has grown to a stage of being physically and emotionally tired; bowels not working, catheter-fitted, each day fraught with courage, pain and unhappiness. She thought she should at least have had a choice. Mother, otherwise a strong, cultured and educated person, outlived her desire for life by four years before she actually died. My brother and I were pleased when she finally and naturally obtained her wish.

My father died quickly one early morning. My mother heard a sharp cry from the bathroom and hurrying, she discovered my father on the floor in front of the toilet. She called her son, Dave, who gave his Dad a half hour of artificial respiration before the paramedics arrived and took him to the hospital where he was pronounced dead from a massive heart attack. No autopsy was performed and no further investigation seemed necessary. We miss him, but Dad had a pleasant death. Am I wrong?

There are infinite stories of death from terminal diseases, starvation, plane crashes, tsunamis, tornadoes, hurricanes, earthquakes, fires, wars, etc. There are as many deaths as fingerprints, and each individual – human, plant and animal – will experience death in a different way.

Which leads me to believe that we have all been given birth by a single mother – the Earth. The Earth is everything's mother, and we are brothers and sisters of the same family. The Earth, with its sun, moon, water, air and thin, permeable crust, is the medium within which we live and the plain facts are that an unimaginable number of all of the planet's former living things are now dead. In fact they make up part of our Earth's crust. They may be part of our topsoil and we may be walking on them.

Thinking about death begs the question of the meaning of life and who cares anyway. First of all, the deceased don't care, because they can't. We have to excuse them.

Does the universe care? What about the grand scale of our universe? The universe, with its big bang 13-1/2 billion years ago, black holes at the center of galaxies, the irrevocable speed of light, the actions of gravity, the prevailing electromagnetic force, the protons and neutrons held together by six quarks and the strong force and the impossible-to-imagine concept of time. Let's face it; the Earth, who gave birth to us and is responsible for us as our mother, we appreciate from that standpoint, but, in the last analysis, the universe has no brain or any other device capable of caring. In other words, there's no evidence it's possible for the universe *to* care.

But, I care about those I love. I might even say, we, as humans, care about those we love. Loving and caring go together. I understand that everything of which I'm aware is miraculous and I *do* value miracles. I care. Humans care. Humans intrinsically understand they are miracles, as are all living objects: plants, birds, fish, mammals, germs, etc., and consequently value and appreciate all the living.

In conclusion: The universe doesn't care whether we live or die. Whether the universe cares or not is meaningless. Humans and everything on this planet are what is meaningful, because, at the moment, we are the best part of the Universe. While our life or death is meaningless to the universe, it's meaningful to every living thing on this planet and we express the miracle of our existence as a whole.

I can visualize the Universe as the Father and the Earth as our mother, and I am a child of the Earth and value the Father. But, for all practical purposes, the Universe, the Father and Mother don't care.

While I'm alive, I value my life as meaningful to me and I care.

Christ Poem

Christ slipped from heaven
In an Aeronca one-eleven
Struck air, then glided
Into one of his storms,
the howling norms.

In a dark thundercloud,
He battled the plane
In tumbling turns
And twists and saves
Until at last,
Perspiration cast,
Zipped out of the clouds
At nine thousand feet.

Grasses below
green and bright,
meandering streams
In cool twilight.
When, fracturing the mind,
The engine sputtered,
And fluttered and died.

But he fought the controls
In twists and turns
Silent and mute,
At four thousand feet
Tripped the plane's parachute
That yanked at the tail
And twisted around.
The only Christ aimed

straight at the ground.

He dizzily plunged
'Til the chute caught the breeze
And yanked the plane
And Christ upright.
The seatbelt, tight.

And there he hung
Facing the ground,
Floating quietly, gently,
Wind on the wings
Whistling and whining,
Lazily approaching
So near to the ground,
The hanging Aeronca
Dangling dangerously
Twisted slowly around.

Lost in the forest
On the tops of the trees
The plane collapsed
In a rumble and tumble,
And a rasp and a smash
Breaking branches,
And scattering birds.
Plane yet vertical
Resting unsteady
Hung by the tail.

And Christ in his belts
Fifty feet from the ground.
bone-dead and tired
He drifted right off

Taking a nap for a
better tomorrow.

(Giving *Christ* a
human contenance)

I Clobber

After reading while Marge is fussing with her new printer, I shut my book, tapping the cover lightly, and observing Marge in deep concentration, I say, in a voice like a pronouncement from God:

I MOVE!
(No response from Marge.)
Again, after a short pause and with *great* import, I say,

I MOVE!
(No response.)
Slowly getting up and turning, I say,

I ARISE!
(Again, no response.)
Then, with greater importance,

I WALK AROUND CHAIR!
(Marge never looks up, just peers at her instructions.)
Spying last night's empty soft drink bottle sitting on the back of the sofa, I say,

I PICK UP BOTTLE!
Marge, glancing briefly, says,

I CLOBBER YOU OVER THE HEAD!

Rider and Elephant

The following was taken from an article found on the Internet that was framed in the nature of a question. What is the **Rider and the Elephant** metaphor?

Jonathan Haight argues that humans have two sides. An emotional/automatic/irrational side (the elephant). An analytical/controlled/rational side (the rider), is rational and can plan ahead.

The elephant is irrational and driven by emotion and instinct. For true success, they must find a balance between the two. Changes often fail because the rider can't keep the elephant on the road long enough to reach its destination.

The elephant's hunger for instant gratification is the opposite of the rider's strength, which is the ability to think long-term, to plan, to think beyond the moment. With the exceptional power of the massive elephant, when rider and elephant move together, changes come easily.

My personal crisis of shortness of breath, inability to fall asleep, feeling of being bloated, and intermittent panic is coincidental with a mental and emotional problem that has chosen to express itself at the same time. Perhaps it is related to my long-term relationship during my early upbringing between me and my mother. My mother has been dead 29 years, and I am in later life and retired from work for five years. Without her, I'd have died. Instead, I lived and was loved.

Eighteen months of age is the time when boys begin to say no and find themselves beginning to individualize into whatever male form they'll be. I suspect I formed an abnormally strong bond with my life-saving mother. I could easily call it the bond of life over death.

I speculate whatever she said could be taken as a profound law and any deviance was accompanied by a look that for a young uninitiated youngster might have had the power of life or death.

My mother or father probably didn't realize this. Being a writer with a journalist for a father, Mother had strong *"rider"* traits. Her elephant was nicely trained. She was given to controlled analysis with an emphasis on words and rationality. Including being literary, she was also an idealist, educated in fine art, music and dance. That's the rider's strong point. She was the apple of her father's eye. Her father was a journalist, foreign war correspondent, and newspaper editor and also had strong rider characteristics.

She loved to write poetry, essays and short stories. I was loved as well as any child could have hoped to be loved, but probably received that love differently because it was linked with a permanent and powerful admonition, *I must listen to her carefully and do what mother wants because she is God and if I don't, I'll die!*

The die was cast! I grew the only way I could without dying. I was mother's boy; either mother's boy, or dead. I had to behave the way mother said because her views had to be my views. My mother was a writer, good with words, educated with plenty of justifications and reasons on why I should think this way or that. My benefit or problem was: I was a *"good"* boy.

Stan Raymond

At 64 and working editor of the Northrup News, Stan is a very likeable fellow. He's tall and slim and carries himself well with a sometimes-wry sense of humor that carries him through. He has three offspring, two of whom are sons, but from time to time one doesn't get along with him. He experienced the unpleasantness of a divorce recently, yet seems to be financially well off and longs to build a new house. He has a definite artistic flair that was heightened and expanded during his early years while studying photography at Art Center. Though at first meeting I experienced him as a conventional person, at times he exhibits a bit of a wild streak, and I suspect he enjoys being somewhat unpredictable.

He looks clean, always shaved with a close haircut, and is always well groomed and seems to like things running smoothly, certainly an asset to his job. As you might expect, his BMW is also in good condition and no doubt well kept. He also has an eye for the ladies, and would probably like to have another intimate, lasting relationship. Through his conversation and the mischievous look in his eyes when he talks about the fairer sex, I know him to be strongly heterosexual. His moral code is such that he respects women and needs to treat them honorably. I never get the impression he would injure them or use them in any way. He's a trusting sort that likes to be exact and is willing to believe what is said, though he's not a fool. His trusting nature, if it were at all detectable, would never blind him to deceit. He is patient to a fault and every time will give the benefit of the doubt to someone who has even the slightest plausible excuse. Regarding money, he's fair in dealing with people and pays those who provide services promptly. He does not like things not wrapped up and always likes to know where things stand.

As an editor, he has an eye for the written word and can

instantly spot improper punctuation marks or a grammatical error. He loves people, and regarding those he respects, is liable to sing their virtues loud and long. There are even overtones of love in his conversations about his closer friends, particularly his chief news writer, Ahmed. I find him to be an optimistic person who sees life, generally, as a good place, though at the moment, he seems lonely and I sense he would like to share his life with a good woman who understands his passions and what he is about.

He can be staunch in the face of adversity. His recent operations were a personal trial, and the significant dental work that was so difficult for him was entered into with resolution and resignation. His father, I'm sure for him, was a tough act to follow. Arthur was a warm, humorous, loved person known for his brilliant aeronautical engineering abilities. He headed one of the foremost aircraft companies during the critical war years, and his genuine talents and ability earned him respect, wealth and a fruitful life. But for his son, Stan, having a father of such strong capability as a continuous role model, and given their relationship was a real one, he benefited and made his own mark according to his own talents. I have observed no competition between them; a mark that is a significant one.

About the house: Despite the fact that his mother is slowly dying of Alzheimer's disease, Stan wants to live in Brentwood next to his father for several reasons. (1) He gets along well with him; (2) The land attached to his father's is his and is a gift from his father. It is almost free and clear; (3) He will eventually inherit his father's house and all the family's belongings; (4) The view, location and environment is sensational; (5) It's a good economic move, because the new lot-split alone is worth $250,000 and he will pay nothing for it; (6) Two houses on it will give him financial flexibility after the inheritance; and (7) He can be near his aging parents and do what he can to be a nearby companion and son who can offer assistance during their later years.

Schooled in photography, Stan has an eye for beauty. At Art Center, he learned to see and was taught composition, color, line and balance, and what makes one artwork beautiful and another not. This inner sense and love of beauty, and his personal sense of integrity are the qualities within him that make him one of those rare, sensitive owners that the better architects continually seek. When doing architectural work, the architect is also trained to make good color, line and composition. I feel that is the mutual quality we have between us that will allow a true, rich, sensitive and mature house to be born. A house can only be the outward expression of the makers. The architect is certainly a maker of houses, but he cannot exist in a vacuum. He is teamed with a new client every time he does a job and it is marvelous to be teamed with someone you can understand and who understands you. In this case, a client who is sensitive, mature, and with an eye for beauty, who has talent and wild qualities. *(In Stan's case, perhaps not latent.)* In thinking about a suitable house for a client such as Stan, a few things come to mind: (A) The site development costs are so high that building a house a few square feet smaller than what it wants to be is a false economy, particularly in a place like Brentwood Village. Oakmont Drive is a community of the successful and well to do; (B) When Stan does inherit the bulk of excellent furniture and memorabilia, he needs a place for it to exist so he can enjoy it; and (C) This house will probably be the final expression of his personal being on this earth, and he has the undeniable right to pursue what that means. Frugality is a worthwhile expression, but a penny-wise, pound-foolish expression is not. Stan and I must seek the balance. I am sure he will restrain himself from rewriting this, though maybe he won't and I'd be glad.

Epilogue: Stan's plans were finished in the latter part of 1987 and the house was in its final stages in the fall of 1988, about the time when the Dodgers were about to win the pennant. Stan had spent Saturdays sitting on his deck in the fresh morning air or in the shade of his unfinished house sipping coffee. He'd *enjoyed* building his house.

One day while in his Dad's house watching the playoff games alone with Arthur *(his dad)* in an adjacent room, Arthur remembers what he thought was a shout of delight from an avid baseball fan. He paid little attention at first, but later the maid discovered Stan dead. An aorta had ripped from his heart sending blood pumping internally. He'd cried out in mortal surprise just before he died.

In 1987-1988, Arthur was about 91, and had sold the upper house and had planned to live with Stan in the new house. He loved his family house and raised his four boys there, collected fine furniture and artworks, and the house held many family memories. Arthur Raymond worked for McDonnell Douglas Corporation and was the chief designer of the DC-3 airplane. Arthur moved into the new house I'd designed for Stan, and when living there, employed me to add a bathroom on the lower floor for he and his new wife. Marge and I were pleased to get Christmas cards with a kind and loving note for his remaining 11 years, until he died in 1998 at 101.

Black Hole

I was shocked. There it was yawning before me! A *black hole!* I'd heard of the theory before, but here it was right before me under the grape arbor with the bird feeder overhead in the center of the spilt birdseeds. Swirls of black dirt were whirling downward and descending to oblivion. I kneeled to get a better look at the black hole and asked myself, *"What's down there?"*

Later in the day, while I was having a grilled cheese sandwich on rye and a glass of milk and reading an astronomy book, I suddenly became aware of movement under the bird feeder near the black hole. The human eye, as I understand it, has a visual sensitivity developed over centuries to detect movements of prey or sneaking enemies. It's called peripheral vision. I turned quickly toward the movement. A creature's nose about the size of a large rat with dim looking eyes was peeking out. In fact, under closer surveillance, he was surreptitiously gobbling bits of bird food from the ground. His eyes looked glazed. I don't think he had vision like the eagle or owls that can detect movement of condemned creatures at great distances or even in the dark. His eyes looked like Mr. McGoo's, in case you remember that visually challenged comic strip character.

I walked quietly out the sliding glass door to take charge and be the alpha dog protector, and do what needs to be done to remove this young intruder, thusly saving future birdseed and my own lawn, which I installed to maintain pristine greenery, enhancing my house and person. The creeping thing retreated to its dark, elongated place of living. I returned to my sandwich and tried to put the horrible thing and its mysterious black hole out of mind. Where does a gopher hole go, anyway?

At two o'clock, I got exhausted and had to take a nap. I lay down on the couch and read for ten minutes, which my mother said was bad for the eyes because lying down with my head positioned so-and-so didn't allow blood flow to my eyeballs, thereby, over the years causing my vision to go bad. She died fourteen years ago at 94, so she doesn't nag me anymore, but sometimes I think she's waggling her finger from the great beyond and going, "Tsk! Tsk! Tsk!" from far away in her own black hole. However, when my eyes can no longer see the page, and my mind begins to wander, and my lids begin to close by themselves, I put the book down, throw a pillow under my knees, put on my bean bag eye shade, made for me long ago for father's day by my eldest daughter, and immediately fall into my own black hole.

Awakening, I gaze outside on the lawn. The neighbor's friendly gray-white cat has detected movement in the hole, and is frozen in place with one relaxed paw slightly lifted. Her attention is full on the black hole and she is instantly ready for an immediate catch. Likewise, I freeze in place watching the cat frozen in place. We are both frozen in place with focused attention on catching the non-appearing creature as it emerges from the black hole. We both wait. Time becomes interminable. After a few minutes the cat sits down and licks its shoulder and walks away. The gopher has long since removed itself from the mouth of the black hole and is pursuing nutrition elsewhere. There is *no way* he'll be caught by a cat knocking on the front door, frozen in an act of foolishness.

A few days later the black hole was filled. Just a high rounded pile of dirt remained. Birds had complete charge of their bird food. The cat being away, I was once more attendant to my own pursuits and momentarily no longer bothered by the **Black Hole.**

Soccer and Lost Dream

I find myself on the second story of what seems to be a sports club. There is a row of wide windows overlooking a broad green playing area. I look out. I assume it's the soccer field. There are lots of young people on the second floor and I am with a male friend who is away somewhere. One soccer team is waiting for the other to arrive. One healthy-looking member is waiting for the game to begin. I say to him, *"I'm anxious to see you run."*

Then it becomes known the other team isn't going to show up. I start to leave and notice the open door of a public bathroom. I go in, lock the door and relieve myself in the toilet. The toilet changes to a 6" round hole in the floor bubbling with clear water. There is a knock on the door and someone wants to get in. Before I'm ready, I stop urinating. I became embarrassed because I was taking too long.

I leave the building, aware that my ex-wife is waiting for me at home. My children are away somewhere, and I'm worried about them, too. My home is still on the promontory below the end of Harbor Vista Drive. The building I am leaving is about six or seven miles north of the Getty Museum on Pacific Coast Highway. I begin walking home and immediately lose the highway or freeway. In searching for it, I find myself walking down a thin, bumpy tiled walkway. *(Like the walkway fronting the new Agoura Hills Trader Joe's Market.)*

Steeply on the left are poor, dilapidated houses. I realize I'm in a poor district and don't feel welcomed. A tall, dark, suspicious looking character comes into view walking toward me at the end of the walk. To my right are worn, bare-looking trees and a side street. Steeply rising beyond the side street is a natural bank that is dark and not inviting. The main highway I need to follow has veered off to an area much higher than the present street.

As I reach the end of the tiled walkway, I see a tree on my left and decide to climb it for a better view. I do so, and notice there is another highway between the main highway and me. It is a narrow, unoccupied highway with no guardrails and still steeply above me. I descend the tree, jumping steeply from dirt to stone until I reach the bottom where I awake.

To Amanda

    Along the tree-lined path she goes.

She bounds and paces, gallops and flows.

    Up to the tops of the mountainous rows

Of boulders and peaks and rolling plateaus.

    A gray shadow blending.

    A dark shadow tending.

To mingle, commingle, combine and compound

    While the fullness and freshness of nature

    abound

While the dew and the drabness of nature surround,

    She slips through the morning with hardly a

    sound.

    A dark shadow tending.

A gray shadow blending

                            Dad

Car Crash in Fog

Marge was awakened Tuesday morning by a screech of brakes and the unmistakable sound of a car crash. She immediately called the Malibu Sheriff and reported the accident, which was at the intersection of Kanan Dume Road and Pitsch/Latigo Canyon Roads near Calamigos Ranch.

At the same time, I was returning from a jog on Kanan Dume, and the strange shape of a dark-colored car loomed quiet and eerie in the center of the road. Coming closer, I saw a parked car on Latigo Canyon Road with a person in the driver's seat attending a standing woman. I asked if she'd called the police and she assured me she had, then the car drove off. Alone, the lady and I stood in the fog. She seemed surprisingly calm, and I asked if she was all right. She said, *"No! She was hurt. Probably a broken thumb."* I looked at her left lower arm that had a bad scrape and a swelling blue welt.

Across Kanan, I was aware of the shadowy presence of someone else helping the other driver. His/her car didn't seem as violently damaged as my lady's car and I, perhaps wrongly, assumed the owner of the other car not so badly injured, even though a wheel had been knocked off and rolled to the shoulder. The whole right front of the looming car and engine owned by the recently-introduced lady had been pummeled to an indescribable mess.

For a few moments, things were silent. I was aware of the fog and a quiet breeze drifting, and decided I'd stay with the lady until help arrived. I assumed she may have needed someone to be with her. I asked if she'd like to sit down. She said, *"No, if I do, I'll faint."* We exchanged our names, then she handed me a camera and asked if I'd be willing to take some pictures. I said, "Certainly," and walked into the street to take a shot in the dim light. To get another angle, I walked to the side of the car only to be missed by another car that flew silently out of the foggy darkness and crashed into the damaged car sending it another 40 feet down the street, and following that one, a fourth car caromed into the back of *him*. Both cars, though damaged, were able to move slowly onto the shoulder. It became blatantly clear we had all the requirements for a multi-car collision.

My lady screamed, *"Stop!"* at a fifth car; the driver, seeing the situation, slammed on his brakes and skidded to a heart-rending stop two feet in front of the damaged car, then pulled around and exited slowly into the fog. I had to admire my lady for understanding the seriousness of the situation and doing all she could to prevent others from disaster by shouting with all her might several times, *"Stop! Stop!"* All told, shouting at oncoming drivers was not going to do the job. They needed a visual warning. I took off my sweatshirt and began waving at approaching cars.

I think I was successful slowing four or five cars until I noticed a blinking red light farther up the road waving the cars down. I ran ahead, and discovered Fred Sabbage, one of the managers of Glen Gerson's Calamigos Ranch. He'd accepted a lighted flare given him by someone, and was flagging people down, though seeing one flare in heavy fog was difficult. We exchanged greetings, and taking two positions about 30 yards apart, we blinked and waved the cars to a stop before they could hit each other. We slowed and stopped 30 to 50 cars, which stacked up upon each other and forced us to advance the distance of our signals. Eventually, there were 400 yards of cars in an uneven line, some moving slowly past, some on the shoulder, some waiting.

After an interminable period, perhaps 20 minutes, a fire engine, paramedic truck, ambulance and a police car arrived with blinking lights. We thought we were done, but still I had to run to the Fire Department and beg the guys to get some flares out right away, which they did.

Everything being under control, I returned to the lady who, by this time, had her arm in a splint and was being put painfully on to a cot to be moved to a gurney, then the paramedic truck.

Worried because I was late coming back from my run, Marge came out looking for me, hoping I was not a victim. I told her I'd been flagging traffic.

The lessons are the same old ones, but they need repeating. Don't follow too closely behind another car, especially when it's foggy and you can't see. If you are forced to stop in a pileup line, pull to the shoulder so the next car won't hit you. Drive with caution on Kanan Dume Road. Glen Gerson and his staff at Calamigos Ranch have assisted crashed motorists for years, and should be given a medal. Marge and I have attended the tragic result of two cars that have skidded on the shoulder and rolled 40' down the embankment to land behind my studio between the live oak trees.

Raindrops on My Face

One evening I fell asleep,
and in a state of anxiety
awakened well after midnight.

I was thinking I had no money.
Our mortgage payment was
two months behind. Our
refrigerator held little food.

High in our master bedroom
I threw off blankets, sat up and
looked out the window over our
short deck with view to the mountain
on the other side of Malibu Creek.

It was pitch black and its ridge
cut sharply across the overcast sky.
Beyond the range of black mountains
and along Pacific Coast Highway
a thin string of lights flickered silently
and now and then winked
while diminishing
all the way to Santa Monica.

In the farther distance five or six
smokestacks from the Hyperion
plant rose above the broader
plane of Redondo Beach.

Huge volumes of steam billowed
from their spouts and moved

soundlessly and aimlessly in the air
before evaporating high in the sky.

Like a distant bee,
a miniature light from a 747
moved slowly and steadily
to a late night landing at LAX.
Karon, my wife, slept soundly.

The children's room was still.
The dog and cats were curled
in their favorite places, at the
foot of the kid's beds. The
night was black and muggy.

I knew of no place to borrow
money nor any place to turn.
I lay in my bed, the back
of my hand on my forehead
and stared at the ceiling.

After a while I dozed off and my
mind drifted to a place in childhood,
where I was eight years old in our
tiny Illinois house in Lombard.

I remembered how safe I felt.
Little brother Dave and I were
in our isolated house in our
diminutive bedroom in the
middle of Lombard cornfields.

We had two Mullberry trees in front,
a detached garage off to the side,

a deep backyard with a well,
and to the rear, a lone Elm tree.

It was also after midnight and I
was sleeping with my head on a
pillow propped against the sill
of a partly opened window.

My mother and father loved me.
I loved them. It comforted me
to smell the soft night breezes
through the slightly opened window.

I listened for a while and in the
distance heard the rumbling of
thunder. A common storm was
rinsing its way across the Midwest,
and would soon pass over our home.

I remember a lull, then a breeze,
a quickly brightened window, then
darkness and a rumble of thunder.

Soon thick droplets struck
our roof, then a rush of rain,
a pause, then more rain.

All through the night an accelerating
roar rattled and danced on the roof.
It gradually increased, softened,
then came with a violence and
sometimes died to a whisper.

It was steady, but the storm was

not as powerful as others. I was
warm and dry and peaceably lulled
to sleep and woke now and then

to experience the spattering of
raindrops on my face and remember
I was where I was and loved.

As this dreamy reminiscence ended
and as a miracle in answer to my
prayers I was awakened by *California
raindrops* lightly striking our roof.

Water from the sky rolled off our roof,
dripped from the eaves, splashed
on the rounded railings and
blackened our deck boards.

A cooler breeze filled our room
and rain whipped and pounded
and caressed our sky-high house.

We were warm and dry
like I was as a child. I sighed
and my eyelids closed.

Rain was a gift from God when
I needed it the most. I thanked the
eternal forces for this welcome
relief, forgot my troubles, and
slept like a contented eight-year-old
for the remainder of the night.

Will the Sun Come Up?

This may seem a simple question. Of course the sun will come up. Have no doubt. As sure as I'm sitting at this keyboard, the sun will come up, though some might ask, how can I *really* be sure? The key word is *REALLY!* They'll accuse me of predicting the future. They'd argue I'd never know 'til tomorrow.

(You may not have time to read this, busy as you are, but I've just retired and have nothing to do anyway so I thought I'd take up this important subject.)

Some might question if I mean will the sun come up *tomorrow*, or continue coming up for a *specified time*, or come up *forever*? Well, *Ex-c-u-u-se ME!* I didn't mean to get into a big argument! I should have entitled my essay, Will the Sun Come up *TOMORROW?* Big deal! Now that's cleared up *(picky-picky)*, so I can go on to other arguments.

It will not come up for *FOREVER!* I kid you not! I've read books and I have it on authority the sun will go out in four or five billion years. *(I don't know where we'll all be at that time, probably heaven, but that's beside the point.)*

We – I use the term *we* because I'm a reasonable man and *we* know it will come up because of past performance. It's always come up every day, so why shouldn't it come up tomorrow?

You might say a storm is approaching from the east, bringing heavy clouds that would hide the sun. Since you couldn't actually *SEE* the sun come up, how'd you know it came up?

This is a ridiculous argument! I'd know it came up because of *LIGHT*. Anybody that would ask that question obviously never heard of light. *(It travels at 186,000 miles per second and takes 8 minutes to arrive from sun to earth.)*

Explaining this piece of information, of course, would probably lead me into more arguments. You might say, *"The sun went out 8 minutes ago and the lack of light wouldn't get here for* about 8 minutes, so how would you know it did not go out?"

I'd immediately counter with, *"There are other sources of light! How about the moon?"*

You'd counter with, *"The moon reflects light from the sun. If the sun goes out, the moon goes out, too."*

"Oh yeah!" I might say, *"I forgot. You have me there. How about starlight?"* (I sent it up the flagpole and nobody saluted.) *"The sun doesn't go out from past experience. It's always come up and there's no reason why it will not come up again. Things are reliable from past performance!"*

"That's no guarantee." You'd say, *"What if you slept in and didn't see it come up? Does that mean it didn't come up while you were sleeping?"* (Why am I arguing with myself?) *"If a tree falls in the forest and no one is there, is there any sound? It's the same thing! If the sun comes up in the morning and no one is there to see it, did it really come up?"*

My friend casts doubt on something I know in my heart is true. Is there no justice? Do all good turns deserve punishment?

Have it your way! OK! Tomorrow the sun WON'T come up!
Anyway

Marbles

(Daughter, Lilianne, to Dad) "So! How was your day?"

"Well, it's been good, so far. I mean, Aaaa, I had French toast for breakfast, and Chris and Morgan came over."

"*Ooooh!*"

"And Morgan had a whole bunch of marbles, and nobody knew how to play marbles, except me, of course. So, Chris and Morgan and I got down on the floor and started playing marbles. I got a little string and put the string on the floor and took our shooters and tried to hit the marbles out, ya know? And, aaa, Chris doesn't know how to shoot marbles at all and Morgan doesn't either, so I was showing them how to shoot marbles."

"*You enlightened them?*"

"Hmmm? What?"

"*You enlightened them?*"

"Yes! I enlightened them. After a little while Morgan didn't think we needed the circle any more –"

"*Oh?*"

"And threw the string away and started to – she just throws the marble at the other marbles. She doesn't play by the rules."

"*Children will often break the rules if they –*"

"You're not supposed to put your hand inside the circle; of course her hands were inside the circle all the time. Chris was playing by the rules, but he couldn't, aaa, shoot the marble with his thumb. Ha! Ha! He didn't know how to do that. Of course, I was raised on marbles and all of a sudden my marble expertise came back."

"*Well!*"

"Ha! Ha! Ha! In the old days, aa – uumm, there weren't that many marbles around and if you went to the store, maybe you could get your mother to buy you some marbles. But they would have maybe a dozen for a dollar or something like that – and then you'd take those to school, and then you'd get into marble shooting games with other kids, and then – if you – the other kids got to keep the marbles that they shot them out of the circle and if they shot out a whole bunch of them, they'd take them home. It wasn't as though you'd get any marbles back from anybody. You could go to school and play marbles and somebody would steal all your marbles! Ha! Ha! That's where the expression *'You've lost your marbles'* comes from! Ha! Ha! Ha! Ha! 'Cause you couldn't get 'em back!"

"*Yeah!*"

"Of course you could always borrow a couple of marbles and win about six or seven and then go home with about eight of the marbles that you'd won, and pay the guy back his two that you'd borrowed to begin with. Anyway, you could do that. D'your kids play marbles?"

"*What?*"

"Do your kids play with marbles?"

"*Sure they do. They have a billion marbles?*"

"They do?"

"*Yeah, they do!*"

"Do they play the marbles game?"

"*No.*"

"They don't *play* marbles?"

"*No. They're more interested in seeing how they can aa aa – you know, see what happens when you drop them in water. You know they don't want to play a game. Cary would like to play –*"

"You have to be nine, I think. You have to be –"

"*A little older –*"

"Nine or ten, – aa – the marble season doesn't really last too long – between nine and eleven and that's about it. Afterward, forget the marbles. Been there, done that. Before you get to be nine, that's –"

"*They want to experiment with them more than they want to*

play. You have to have the spirit of larceny in your blood."
"He! He! He!"
"You have to want to win something!"
"He! He! You have to have the gambler's spirit. You have to want to put a quarter in the slot machine and pull the little handle and watch all the little plums and lemons and cherries go "Bct! Bct! Whheeww!" Of course, if you don't win, you've lost your dumb quarter. Dumbkoff! Ha! Ha! Ha! Ha! Ha! But, if you have that kind of spirit, then play marbles. Because in those days, you know, it was definitely competition. If you lost all your marbles, you'd go crying all the way home. Ha! Ha! Ha! That would be fun, huh? Ha! Ha!"
"Yeah! Sort of."
"Huh?"
"Nostalgic!"
"I'm going to have to do a piece on marbles. What the old marble thing was all about, you know?"
"Well, didn't people have to collect marbles, too? A certain kind of marbles?"
"In any marbles – in the OLD days, there were certain marbles that were very special. They had a special aura! I mean, they just had the stuff! They had the juice! There were knicks –"
"Yeah! I know –"
"K-N-I-C-K-S and there were – I don't know – there were some with names – with some that were perfectly clear glass, and they'd be perfectly clear red, green or yellow and then there were multicolored marbles, and then there were all black marbles and all the marbles were different sizes and your shooters – to be a good shooter, your marble always had to fit your hand, it would have to be the perfect size –
"Well, I –"
You could shoot 'em faster, farther. You should be able to shoot the marble and the marble would just stick, and the other marble would fly out of the circle about 10', and your little

shooter would just sit there and spin, in one spot, you know? And wherever your shooter would stop, you would be able to shoot from there – and a lot of times, if you'd stick in one spot, you'd be close to the other marbles and you could knock all the marbles out. If your marble shooter also went out of the circle with the marble that you'd hit, then, of course you'd have to stay outside the line, then you could shoot – move around the circle, and shoot from any direction you wanted –" *(Yawn!)* "– to try to knock the marbles out. You could even hit two marbles or you could knock three out at one time."

"You mean . . . ?"

"If there were three of them in there, you could line up two marbles and get a shot to knock both marbles out of the circle. If you could get your shooter to stick in there, you could then shoot 'em all out! Ha! Ha! Ha! And, you know, a really good marble player could clear up the whole marble pot in one turn, you know. He would dump six marbles in there and you'd dump your six in there and you do hands, like one, two, three, with one finger or two fingers, and one guy would call evens or odds and one would say odds and if the fingers were odd, he'd get to go first. If a guy called even, and the fingers were even –"

"Yeah!"

"Then you'd get to go first. So then the first guy would get the first shot, and frequently he'd knock them all out and you'd go home crying. Ha! Ha! Ha! Ha! You Dumbkoff!! Ha! Ha! Ha!"

"Roy! Really!"

"Ha! Ha! Ha! I hope you're not doing anything now, but – Ha! Ha! – self esteem and athleticism came into it too, and some guys were stronger shooters and were able to shoot the marbles at a faster rate. And they could – ah – there were problems – aa – and there were others whose fingers weren't quite as strong, or they didn't have the competitive spirit, or couldn't play as well, and they'd lose their marbles pretty quick and –"

"He! He! He!"

"Ha! Ha! Ha! And they'd go home crying! Ha! Ha! Ha! I want my marbles! And the mother would say –"

"OOOooooooo!"

"Oh! I'll buy you some new ones. Ha! Ha! Ha!"

"*Life was so much simpler then.*"

"Ha! Ha! Ha! Ha! Ha! That's all we did! We had nothing else to do! Well, like – just play marbles! Ha! Ha! Ha! You didn't have to worry about work! Raising money! Buying a house! Ha! Ha! Ha! Ha! Ha! This marble thing was really important – that was when there were only 150 million people in the United States."

"*Oh, really –*"

"Now there's like, 300 million. Isn't that amazing?"

"*Yeah, it is.*"

"And the U.S. is one of the most sparsely populated countries."

"*Yes, it is.*"

"China has, ah, billions of people – China – Jakarta is highly populated – Germany, right near Belgium, is absolutely jammed wall to wall!"

"*I know.*"

Like they've got a big bunch of houses where the Black Forest was. Ha! Ha! There ain't no Black Forest anymore! The Black Forest is like, pavement! Ha! Ha! Ha! So that's what I was doing with all my morning so far."

"*Well, that sounds wonderful!*"

"Ha! Ha! Ha! Ha! Ha!"

Another Recent Episode

The father organism is on his hands and knees on the floor of the family room, happily ironing the rug and singing *Whistle While You Work,* when his teenage daughter, on her way out, hits him in the head with her purse, knocking him ever so slowly, knees over T-shirt, into the corner where he eventually comes to rest, surprised with hair over his eyes.

Later, to Marge, the father organism says, *"Now, why did she do that?"*

Washing dishes, Marge replies, *"You were ironing the family rug with the clothes iron."*

"I know, the father replies, *but it wasn't plugged in."*
Heavy sigh.

The Spider in the Sink

This morning, when I came back from my morning run, I found a spider in the sink. He couldn't get out and became exhausted with attempts to escape. What was he doing in the sink? Was he thirsty? Do spiders get thirsty? How do they drink? What does their mouth look like? I guess I'd have to put him under a microscope, if I had one, to find out what spiders' mouths look like. Of course, I could look up spiders on the Internet or buy a spider book. There must be easily accessible information on spider mouths.

Enough cogitation on spiders and their mouths! What was I going to do with him, squash him with a paper towel and throw him in the trash? Flush him down the sink? Flushing would be hard because the spigot stream couldn't reach him. If I did manage to flush him down, I imagine him riding the surge of a swirling event horizon to his personal black hole where all that awaited him was continuously flowing water down a dark tube to oblivion. Exhausted, he'd probably hang on in cataclysmic terror until ignominious death by drowning.

He was also a fellow creature, his genus having arrived millions of years before mankind was one of the living entities that, when we've all died, was intended to inherit the earth. Do I have the authority to snuff out the life of such an important creature? Not that I'd needed permission. I *am* my own boss and nobody's boss over me!

Eventually, I was going to have to stop running, turn around and face the tiger. That is, decide for myself. Then the thought hit me about what I'd been telling Marge about ants and spiders. Marge has been exasperated and angry about ants and spiders in the house. When a pioneering ant with cocky singleness of purpose crawls on her plate, she throws a fit and tries to flick him off, but in so doing he fastens himself to her finger, but then the ant, in order to withstand the violent accelerating forces raging on the tip of her finger, hunkers down and holds on until she manages to brush him into the wastebasket.

I've seen a clump of ants on the rug with others staggering miles behind climbing and falling over the unevenness of our beige carpet fibers, brim-full of motivation, making their impossible journey to surround, bump into each other, head in the wrong direction, say, "Oops! I'm sorry!", get on course and carry off their infinitesimal portion of cookie crumb back across the same ridiculous pathway. From there, they mechanically file outside through an invisible hole under the doorsill, across 14,000 miles of cement patio to a never-to-be-seen-by-the-human-eye anthill.

But as I was telling Marge about ants, "You know, ants live here, too. We share our space with ants. They were here first. We built *our* house over *their* anthill. We've invaded *their* territory; the least we can do is share the space."

Marge grumbles and reluctantly agrees because different views on ants aren't worth discussing. I decide to let the spider crawl on a paper towel I've just ripped off the roll which he conveniently, and I presume appreciatively, does. As I walk out the back door to our covered patio, he's immediately lost in a paper fold, mind blown and abandoning himself to fate. There, I place the paper with the spider in it on a glass table. He's small enough that while I'm carrying him I have no fear he'll dart out and bite my thumb, injecting some rare poison that throws me into a painful, hallucinatory and perhaps psychotic death-shock.

I wait a few seconds to see if he'll run out from the paper fold and leap off the table into space, probably trailing a silky line to the cement slab, and hightail it across the cement to the safety of ground cover. But he stays under the fold. He's no doubt still unhinged and needs time to recover after a traumatic event like just having been saved from certified death by watery sink.

I go to breakfast thinking, "I wonder how he'll do, now he's outside on the table? Did I do him any favors? If he thinks of it, he can walk to the edge of the table, down it's edge and under the table walking upside down until he reaches a leg, then down the leg to the cement and away across the top of the slab. Not that I know why, but I questioned myself if he had planned a logical escape route. I feel good having saved the life of a little spider creature. Maybe he'll leap off into space trailing a web string and escape."

What am I doing? I don't have to decide for the spider. The spider has to stop running, turn around, and face his own tiger. We *all* have to stop, turn around, and face our own tigers!

Where will he go?

Maybe his survival requires he be *inside* the house. Have I merely *delayed* a spider death? Is the road to hell *always* paved with good intentions? Is it true no good deed goes unpunished? Does the spider now have to face the frigid outside air only to be discovered later with legs doubled over and body rolled into a little brown ball, cold, alone, uncared for; a pathetic little nothing-lump in a crack in the cement?

I returned. He'd gone. He was alive. Where did he go? Probably made a beeline for the back door.

Over and Under

When will the –
>   ***When.***
In the time of the oval-shaped moon
>   ***At some strange time***
Edge dipped in blood and swollen,
>   ***Of adversity and challenge***
Let out the stars
>   ***Shall we know the truth.***
In their infinite right
>   ***That can only be right.***
To spread, engulfing
>   ***A truth that incorporates***
Proclaiming, encompassing
>   ***Everything***
And when they have found
>   ***And when the truth is known***
And permeated
>   ***And we feel it***
And infiltrated
>   ***In our minds***
And claimed
>   ***And hearts***
Then the right is theirs
>   ***Then we know truth***
And theirs alone
>   ***Irrevocably.***
And they remain solid
>   ***Forever.***
Immovable
>   ***Unyielding.***
And glow with a certainty
>   ***And brightened in glory***
Unequaled by men

Over and Under

    That knows no bounds.
They are
    Stars exist
They claim
    In their particular place
They do
    Glowing and radiating
For the stars are of the earth
    For stars are truth.
And none can dig under
    And nothing digs under truth
For they are under
    For truth is changeless
As well as over
    Wherever it is
And it would do well
    And it is necessary
To ponder this thing
    We think on this thing
And take heed
    And understand
And absorb this absolute fact
    So it is absorbed within
Into our beings
    And incorporated completely
So that none can dig under us
    So we can be like stars
For, we are also under
    And know the truth
And over, if once we see the stars
    As stars know the truth
As they truly are.
    And we know the truth.

Secular Viewpoint

Easy Things

I believe the sun will come up tomorrow because: I've lived for over 80 years, and during that time I have been there while it comes up day after day.

One time, our dance group hiked to the top of Bony Ridge Mountain, and we sat among the morning grasses and watched the sun creep silently above the horizon. It was magnificent! It has a good track record. It's been doing that for 4-1/2 billion years. I believe the sun will come up in the morning.

Consider the moon, too. All my life I've observed the moon going through its normal phases, zero to crescent to quarter to half to three-quarters and finishing with a glorious, outstanding full moon, illuminating all the windblown wheat fields and the tops of pine forests. In the full moon's night, animals roam the darkness to feed, and snakes slither in the night for food, purposefully as in a dream. As an after-dinner hoot, owls begin at 4:30 A.M. With yellow eyes, mountain lions prowl stalking prey. I believe in the rising moon.

I believe in rainstorms, snowstorms, sleet, fog, and clouds, wind, hurricanes, tornadoes, and dust storms because I've either experienced them or seen them on TV.

I believe in TV because I can see the screen, and I believe in computers and transportation systems, like a car, because I have driven in one to Staples.

I believe in ocean pollution, diminishing sharks, shellfish and barrier reefs, air destruction, clear-cut forests, lessening oil reserves, melting icebergs, wars, starvation, genocide, poverty, exploitation, extinction of human and animal species; selfishness, greed, mammon, zero compassion and what seems an almost complete disregard for the world, including plants, animals and minerals.

I believe in do-gooder organizations such as the Red Cross,

Salvation Army, Goodwill Industries, The Sierra Club, Cystic Fibrosis Foundation, Habitat, Feed the Children, American Cancer Society, and Meals on Wheels, Aid to American Veterans, and those individuals who have compassion for the increasingly pathetic condition of the world.

The Universal Force

But it's easy to believe in things right in front of your face. But what about the concept of God, the ambivalence toward organized religions, the arguments for and against abortion, the paranormal, natural evolution, politics, life after death?

I believe in a Universal Force, some may call God, that allowed all of which we are aware and all of which we are *not* aware to exist.

Imagine the Big Bang; beginning at a point so small scientists call it *"singularity"* and then with an explosion so immense, it created the whole universe and everything in it of which we know and don't know.

Within an immense empty space that's so large, expanding dimensions are only relative distances between physical bodies that are continually changing.

Now draw an imaginary line around the whole universe, and notice our galaxy is wherever you'd like it to be, and our planet is within that galaxy, also inside that circle. Notice, too, that *we* are on our planet and this forces us to admit we are a small extension of the Big Bang. *"Star stuff!"* as Carl Sagan would call it. I am part of the Big Bang whether I choose to be or not! Everything is the result of the Big Bang, and I, and all plants, animals and minerals are part.

Parallel lines, like railroad tracks, never meet. I have to accept that fact.

Cutting things in half to find the smallest building block of the universe continues over and over again until all that is left is another portion to divide. I have to accept that fact.

I can always add one to the largest number I'm capable of imagining.

If a God, great in his purpose, designed the Big Bang, I have to ask who made that God and who made the second God, and third, ad infinitum until what is left is only another question, who made that one? I have to accept that fact.

Parallel lines that eventually meet, or the division of things resulting in a singular building block, or discovering the one and only final God is completely unreasonable, is one more fact I have to accept.

It is reasonable to believe that some things in my universe have no finite solutions. Some things are insoluble things.

What is, is! And whether I think it's a miracle or not, I have to accept that fact, too.

There are questions I have with absolutely no answers from me or any living creature to be found.

Life After Death

I bought a refrigerator and was told the light goes out when I closed the door. Imagining no other way to test the state of the light, how would I really know the light was out when I closed the door?

I took a chair and sat so that I could get a close look at the edge of the refrigerator door. I watched it very carefully while closing it with keen eyesight and was unable to see if it really went out. I came away with no closure; no assurance that I was not wasting electricity or time. I wasn't sure whether it went out or not and have reached no indication either way; no sign of relief that I know what's happening.

If my life were the refrigerator and closing the door was death and the man told me the light *(my life)* was supposed to stay on and, perhaps, be more brilliant than before, how could I be sure?

Some of those who've had near-death experiences are

convinced there is life after death; however, they were still alive when they came to know that truth. They weren't dead like the raccoon killed and prone on the highway for a few months quickly returning to dust.

When people like my mother and father have passed beyond to unequivocal death, and, let's say, after a couple of years, how do I know they are still living the good life in the hereafter? I don't!

What then is this *"through eternity"* everyone talks about? There is no eternity except the large, small, or medium changes that a particular person left, minimally or maximally, upon our present day world. Thank you, Edison. Thank you, Mr. Ford. Thank you, Mark Twain.

The condition is similar to parallel lines that never meet, the division of matter resulting in yet something to divide, and being assured that one Deity is the absolute and final God that made everything, I can never know and I have to accept that fact.

Serious Prayer

Serious praying is profound hope that calls out to all known and unknown sources of aid.

Praying your child recovers from a severe illness or that you don't get killed or injured in the war or your leaking boat stays afloat until you reach shore are worthy of serious prayers.

For all serious problems, I would pray to beneficial forces for my recovery, such as doctors, nurses, high-end equipment, family, and others willing to aid and making up the useful portion of the Universal Force.

If I call the Universal Force "God," I would be praying to God.

Prayer is making it known I need help. It's possible I may never know the source of what aids me, but the more signals I send, the more help I pray I might get.

The more the appeal to those that can help me, the better.

More loving brains are better than fewer loving brains. Advertising helps!

As Ted Turner's father told him, *"Early to bed, early to rise, work like Hell and advertise."*

"Pray to God, but keep your powder dry. Don't pray to God to keep your powder dry for you."

Unserious Prayer

To win the big game, forces have to be in place and team members must be healthy, motivated, and well-practiced. There's a difference between reasonable and unreasonable praying. If team members are unhealthy, unmotivated and unpracticed, reasonable praying degenerates into wishful thinking. Even if it's really hard, wishful thinking rarely helps.

Reincarnation

The theory that a person can die, then come back as the same person falls w-a-a-a-y out of any theory of common sense. In order to believe that, modern science must be totally neglected as so much nonsense. The first to go is the miracle that no two humans in existence in the world are the exactly same. Why? Because a man's single ejaculation of millions of semi-similar sperm at arbitrary times fighting for a random chance of penetrating an always different female egg, is impossible to pick or choose. This is continually being proved, moment-to-moment, throughout mans' and womens' lifetime. Two different men and women as father and mother at an earlier time will not be the same as two men and women at a later date; therefore, they will not provide the identical sperm and egg as the first one being considered. In order for that to happen, there would be similar beings in enough crowds to be readily noticeable. This is not the case.

Were it so, the circumstances of the world would differ as time passes, and over a 60 or 70 year lifetime, conditions would be so different that the proper responses, human to human, would not be the same in a later century. Correcting mistakes as *"lives"* go on would be impossible, because the conditions would not be the same for the new lives.

What and Why Pictures

I received an Easter Seals catalog today that had many beautiful close-up pictures of flowers: lilies, tulips, narcissus, zinnias, etc. What came to mind immediately was they are what I call *What* pictures. That is, there is no mistaking the photographer's intentions as to what his pictures are. They are pictures of flowers! They fall into the common category of almost all pictures taken by professionals and amateur alike. They are pictures of *What* the subject is. Pictures of exotic fish, gorgeous as they are, are *What* pictures. There's no doubt in the photographer's mind what he is trying to show, nor is there any doubt in the viewers mind as to what he or she is looking at: exotic fish! What are you showing me here? Flowers and fish, defined herein as a *What* picture.

What pictures may be poorly or expertly composed and may be extraordinarily or boringly represented. Certainly the award winning portrait of the Afghan girl with arrestingly green eyes featured on the cover of National Geographic is one of the most loved and moving pictures in the world. It should be in the Hall of Fame for Pictures. Or the historic 1903 pictures of the Wright Brothers' first airplane flights at Kitty Hawk are both beautiful and nostalgic. We need *What* pictures to record history, remember things nostalgically, and have our minds emblazoned with items so far-flung as old wedding pictures and holocaust pictures. There's no refuting the personal or historic value of *What* pictures.

What pictures also have connotations. A bird has connotations of flight, lightness, air, freedom, nesting, eggs, a variety of colors, etc., plus all the connotations people bring to the picture of a bird. The subject or subjects of a picture are its connotations and to simplify it, I call connotations the *agenda*. All *What* pictures have a story to tell or connotations or an *agenda*. An example would be a picture of a kitten playing with a string. It's cute and I take vicarious enjoyment of the kitten's process. A lion, on the other hand, running hard after a frightened wildebeest, tells me I'm going to avoid facing African challenges. What I take from a *What* picture is *What* the picture is of, and the connotation or the *agenda* elicited by the subject.

Most photographers, amateur and professional alike, shoot *What* pictures. Some are good and some are bad and they are all subject to the *agenda* or story about what they are photographing. Marge and I have a beautifully framed photograph of a young mother and her first child taken by a photographic professional friend of mine. I wouldn't trade it for the world. It's a *What* picture with connotations of a mother's love for her first born, my own children, when they were young, how my wife looked with our babies, etc. It's a wonderful *What* picture with strong personal meaning and very precious to me.

But, what are *Why* pictures? A *Why* picture is an arbitrary name I've given to any photograph where the subject or subjects do not directly telegraph the subject's agenda; where the point of the photo is not simply the subject and connotations of the subject; where the a picture of a mother and child may be augmented in how its photographed that adds mystery, irony, strangeness or impossibility to understanding. One that leaves questions, or shows another way of seeing, or allows the picture to have an incongruity or different perspective.

Examples:

Example of a *What* picture: A turn-of-the-century streetcar in the middle of the street parked on its tracks with passengers entering and wires connected to overhead power lines. The picture is historic, well-composed and shows the expertise of the photographer in capturing his subject. It has connotations of early century public transportation and records the city life of the inhabitants.

Example of a *Why* picture: A picture taken at a public harbor through a plate glass window showing the inside of a restaurant with customers happily eating and chatting. But superimposed in the plate glass through which the photo was taken is a shadowy reflection of a passerby at a much larger scale. The large dark man is seen as a commanding figure looming over the restaurant people, while behind him sailing ships with tall masts are reflected.

The agenda of the *What* picture is easily understood by the known value of each of its objects. The agenda of the *Why* picture creates questions, or a mystery, or a lack of continuity, and the viewer has to ask *Why*. At least three things are happening. (1) People at normal scale eating lunch; (2) A ghostlike superimposition of a foreboding man out of scale and too large for people shown smaller; and (3) Including a background of sailing ships and masts. With this going on the viewer is left with the question, *Why?*

This whole essay is to point out two ways of seeing pictures: *What* pictures, that can be understood through logic, remembering and common sense, and *Why* pictures that defy perfect understanding, incomplete by introducing discontinuity, feeling and unanswerable questions.

Birthday Thoughts

Well, here I am. I made it to 84 years old. Last night, Marge threw me a party with Amanda and the boys, Chris Lewi, Tom and Viv, and Ernie and Camille. There was much laughter and talking and good humor. Everyone seemed to have a good time. I got two books from Marge that I picked out with her at Barnes and Noble. One by Bill Cosby called *I Didn't Ask to be Born (but I'm glad I was),* and another by Alexander McCall Smith, *Unforgettable Memories of Youth.* Chris gave me a political birthday card written to confuse, Amanda baked me an apple pie, and Viv and Tom will take us to see *The Artist,* a movie with a musical soundtrack and subtitles, but no audible words. I'll let myself know how it turns out the day after tomorrow.

How did I feel about yesterday and how do I feel about my birthday today? I feel a lot of things. I feel a *plethora* of things. Chuck Hazlewood, my old and good friend from my first architectural job in Denver, said in a birthday letter that with my involvement in writing, artwork, and architecture, my head must be whirling with a lot of stuff. He doesn't know I've read about 36 books a year or more for the past ten years. Reading keeps my mind active because I'm constantly removing portions of my personal ignorance. Of course, there's no end to anyone's personal ignorance, and yes, it's probably true that my head is filled with many things, hopefully only one thing at a time. But there is a benefit to that, because the basic tenets of art, writing and architecture are closely intertwined. What is true for one is generally true for the other.

I have a more than my share of interest in the cosmos. That is, the big bang, stars, planets, nebulae, galaxies, the electromagnetic fields, black holes, Higgs field, and the invisible presence of dark matter and dark energy. I also am involved with tiny things like protons, neutrons, electrons, quarks, and neutrinos. I also enjoy how the brain works philosophically and psychologically and why people think weird things. I am disturbed that the Christian Bible, Jewish Bible, and Koran have differing viewpoints that worshippers take so seriously. It seems they all have forgotten tolerance. If someone is not of his or her group, they are considered an outsider and it's ultimate philosophy is it's us against them. It seems a great portion of people who are adamantly involved with one group or another can never understand the viewpoint of a different group. Even to the extent of having an animosity toward any group not theirs, usually leading to conditions of war. I see little hope for agreement, even though all children of the world – black, white, yellow, etc. – are all the same when they arrive out of the womb, They seem to be ready to be warped according to their parents' beliefs and those of their local environment.

Then I must add that I am concerned with the population explosion, which has doubled in the past 50 years, the diminishing ozone layer, the massive melting of Greenland and the icebergs, the proliferation of oil products producing vast quantities of carbon dioxide, the demolition of natural forests, the only habitat of animals that produce life-giving oxygen, the massive extinction of animal species, pollution of the ocean by oil spills and idiotic non-intelligent fishing methods, the rapidly growing need for clean, fresh water, and the fact that over half the earth's population lives in a state of poverty.

So, where does that get us? Where does that get me? There seems little I can do about the earth's problems. Reading the book called, *How it All Ends,* tells of the end of the Universe. I have learned that our planet will survive its lack of function for another four billion years before it's enveloped by an expanding sun. Other reading tells me that if our privileged planet were to start all over again, it may not have developed a creature as intelligent and creative as a human. The dinosaurs lived for over 135 million years until their extinction 65 million years ago, when a comet hit the Yucatan peninsula and the world had its fifth extinction. If it had missed the earth, dinosaurs might still be ruling the planet, and little mammals would be living in holes to avoid extinction.

It is my philosophy that life must be lived in process and context. We'll build a hybrid car because gas prices are too high. Building a gas-guzzler when fuel is limited doesn't work. If I'm living according to my philosophy, I want to live the process of my life within the context of what's going on around me. Let's face it. I made it to 84. How am I? I'll tell you. I don't have the energetic body I had when I was 10 years younger. My kids are 10 years older. Things have changed with children and friends since time is change.

So! It's time to go with Marge and have a chile relleno.

For What is Thanksgiving?

As was frequently so,
my alter ego held the floor.
It said,
Doesn't everyone have need?
Where shall we go?
If I must, I will!
Well, of course,
this was no answer!
As I suspected
my alter ego
was a complete void!
Perhaps the **Will-o-the-Wisp**
could shed some light.
I called the bard
and put it to him, thus,
"Hi there! **Will**, baby!
for what is thanksgiving?
Will was silent!
Without a word,
hands in pockets,
he examined the ground.
Again, I cried,
"**Will**, *my friend!*
Alligator got your tongue?
Mind stagnant from
over-pondering?
In desperate need
of sustenance,
or need a roll, perchance,
or a spot of coffee?
Maybe the rain

through universal magic
will succor you
to see the light."
For two days I waited.
Will-o-the-Wisp
spoke not a word,
but when he did
he poured forth
with fluttering eyes
reams of utterance,
and bumbling lips,
like a traveling train
at reckless speed until
his excessive language,
swamped my mind,
and it took me moments
to gather it in,
to understand,
to settle it out.
For what is thanksgiving?
The gist was,
"When the rosebud blooms
on the fifth of December,
and morning glories
sing their noonday song,
then tiny beetles will
cross lonely paths
and make their way
through Tom,
the philosopher's
abandoned garden,
and then he paused.
. . . . .
and asked,

What was the question?
I say,
Is this a joke?
Will-o-the-Wisp
speaks in strange codes.
As everyone knows,
he elucidates in riddles.
A friend, the Elephant,
agreed and said,
*"Beware the **Will-o-the-Wisp!***
With fearsome mallet
and powerful drives
he'll pound the ground
and mangle the earth
to claim his space!
Was **Will** under pressure,
temporarily gone mad,
a pot, seething to boil,
a gift in the closet
waiting to be given,
a punch-line pregnant
to pounce,
a teetering rock
ready to plummet?
But, I digress.
More reasonably,
his answer struck me so,
a question, undisturbed,
hanging in the air.
We'll think again
and take another tack.
I have a passionate pal
on a fanatical journey
in search for silence

For What is Thanksgiving?

who laughs at whales
at freezing depths,
while in his mind
on a journey
to Mercury, Venus and Mars,
but won't be back
'til Thursday.
Then!
While a stinging meteor
bulleting through outer space
and tumbling it's ragged way
to maim an astonished earth,
another idea strikes me.
What about my nemesis the **Crow?**
I'll ask him what I want to know.
For what is thanksgiving?
The **Crow** on the wire
casts a cynical eye,
while observing cats,
climbing his cliff
and then leaps off,
and flying a circle,
before settling, again.
Would **Crow** have a notion,
a planetary vision,
a thought from the ether,
an idea from the sky
of the workings of things?
I'll call to him to see.
*Do you have a moment
to fill me in?"*
Crow raised his head,
ruffled his feathers,
looked at the clouds,

and with a gravelly throat,
yawned and cawed
then, as a fowl, he spoke.
"Beware the tide,
it's on the rise,
coming in, and
won't be denied!"
Then leaped in the air
and with a flap or two
was over the forest,
in fading sun,
a lonely dot
lost forever.
So much for **Crow**!
Where's **Will-o-the-Wisp?**
Is he gone again?
Once he said,
"Observe the young girl
dancing in the moonlight
while night breezes
high in the trees
sing intimate songs
and well-worn stones
dimly in light
of a mellowing moon
give warmth
to creatures beneath
while dreaming
of times gone by.
When all's said and done,
what's to become ... ?"
There he is again!
I asked him,
Will-o-the-Wisp,

For what is thanksgiving?
He replied,
"Not until yesterday
or even tomorrow
will the night bird
claim it's hazy space,
nor will the elephant,
in longevity and peace,
walk it's dithering way.
For never fear,
everything will ... "
And he ended it there
then closed his eyes
and fell asleep
and left me
hanging in air.
I was beside myself!
And that's a trick,
for I'd need two selves,
one to be here,
one to be there!
What's the answer
when naught is a non-entity
and nothing is nowhere to be found?
A **Dragon** materialized!
What's this odd creature
occupying this strange space?
Is he a dream?
Am I dreaming?
A menacing growl.
A kick of the leg.
A throwing of flames
in a powerful voice
the dragon spewed forth

> the strangest of words,
> **AAARRRGGGHHHUUUHHHGGG?**
> I couldn't make it out.
> but asked him;
> **For what is thanksgiving?**
> The **Dragon**
> uttered and stammered
> and worried
> and tried to explain
> and became so
> unbearably shy
> that into the fog
> he almost disappeared
> but gathered his courage,
> rallied and told me the answer.

That which makes our hearts sing *is our gift, and we shall accept freedom as our right as the wind surrounds the planet. It gathers in storms and hurricanes or blows in zephyrs across the desert wildflowers. The wind is pure and simple and infinitely renewed by the racing planet, the freshness of the vast waters and growing things. We enjoy the air that is cleaned and furrowed by the sharp and glistening points of mountains.*

We are thankful, as the wind, to be free. And as the wind we have power, strength, sensitivity and appreciation.

In love, we are free to live and give. See here now, this is the way **To live! To grow! To be!**

If we do, won't the air be ridden with thunderstorms and stabbed with lightning bolts? Won't hurricanes hurl throngs of salt water droplets at the seashore towns and cities? Won't the Payne's Gray underbelly of the clouds in its vastness be spectacular? Won't the immense cloud light up and glow from its interior, with curved gray shadows giving it form, volume and dimension?

Won't our loved ones share this bounty and be with us in love at this very special, but intimate time on our miraculous planet?

We are all part of this natural force and feel its being as our own and give Thanksgiving for the security and warmth of our family and this intimate, planetary closeness and Universal love.

Other Books by Doug Rucker

Personal Journey
    Poems predicting next phase of life
Early Stories
    Autobiography – Birth through University
Groundwork
    Autobiography – Marriage to office opening
Growing Edge
    Autobiography – Office opening to Recreation complex
Moving Through
    Collection of poems with *"No Think"* pastels
Book of Words
    Essay collection – Humor & philosophy
Harold and the Acid Sea of Reality
    Thoughts on fantasy & reality
Trial by Fire – A Tale of Two Houses
    Burning and rebuilding of home
Building a Home that Loves You
    Philosophy of architecture with pictures
Transitions
    Realism, Realism & Reflections, Abstract
Thinking in the Abstract
    Deciphering abstract art
Poetries
    Abstract Art, Poetry, Prose

Brief Biography

Born in Elmhurst, Illinois, a suburb of Chicago, Doug was educated at the University of Illinois in Champaign-Urbana. In January of 1950, he obtained his Bachelor of Science degree in the school of Architecture, and in Denver, became a draftsman in a small architectural firm. Moving through Tucson to San Diego, he worked a year for a larger firm doing schools, while weekends he swam in the ocean and dived for abalone. In Altadena, he married and obtained his California architectural license, and pursued his architectural goals as a draftsman in Pasadena and Glendale. Moving to Santa Monica, he continued drafting in a small architectural firm in Brentwood Village, where eventually he was promoted to *"designer."* In 1955, he built his first house in Santa Monica Canyon and immediately sold it, then built a second house and sold that while moving into the first one that had quickly come up for sale.

In the Santa Monica Canyon years, his wife gave birth to three marvelous daughters, and by January of 1958, he opened his first permanent office as an architect operating solely in Malibu. In 1966, he moved his family into a new Malibu architect's dream house overlooking Surfrider Beach. Four years later, it burned to the ground and it took him two more years to build a more fire-resistant house over the same foundations. The new house remains, and has been noted in *Gebhardt and Winter's Los Angeles Guide to Architecture*. His Hogan house was designated a Cultural Historic Landmark by

the City of L. A. Cultural Heritage Commission.

Doug has spent most of his career doing new houses and additions in Malibu and local areas, but has also taken on single jobs in Kauai, Greece, Denver, Fallbrook, Barstow, and Long Beach, and did eight projects in Santa Barbara. In 1980, he was divorced from his first wife, and married Marge Lewi-Rucker, who had four kids of her own. All are grown and deeply into their own lives. Marge is deceased, and Doug now lives a contented life in Malibu on a landscaped acre in a small house of his own design. Retired from architecture, he brings a special passion to writing and photographic digital art.

www.ingramcontent.com/pod-product-compliance
Lightning Source LLC
Chambersburg PA
CBHW040801150426
42811CB00056B/1126